Just The Facts101 Textbook Key Facts

Custom Microsoft Office 2013

Malcolm X

Textbook NOT Included

Table of Contents

Title Page

Copyright

Foundations of Computer Science

Computers

Human-computer interaction

Software engineering

Computer security

Theoretical computer science

Information technology

Database management

Artificial intelligence

Computer networking

Index: Answers

Just The Facts101

Exam Prep for

Custom Microsoft Office 2013 Malcolm X

Just The Facts101 Exam Prep is your link from
the textbook and lecture to your exams.

**Just The Facts101 Exam Preps are unauthorized and comprehensive reviews
of your textbooks.**

All material provided by CTI Publications (c) 2019

Textbook publishers and textbook authors do not participate in or contribute to these reviews.

Just The Facts101 Exam Prep

Copyright © 2019 by CTI Publications. All rights reserved.

eAIN 1469113

Foundations of Computer Science

Generally speaking, computer science is the study of computer technology, both hardware and software. However, computer science is a diverse field; the required skills are both applicable and in-demand across practically every industry in today's technology-dependent world.

:: Transaction processing ::

_____ is the maintenance of, and the assurance of the accuracy and consistency of, data over its entire life-cycle, and is a critical aspect to the design, implementation and usage of any system which stores, processes, or retrieves data. The term is broad in scope and may have widely different meanings depending on the specific context even under the same general umbrella of computing. It is at times used as a proxy term for data quality, while data validation is a pre-requisite for _____ . _____ is the opposite of data corruption. The overall intent of any _____ technique is the same: ensure data is recorded exactly as intended and upon later retrieval, ensure the data is the same as it was when it was originally recorded. In short, _____ aims to prevent unintentional changes to information. _____ is not to be confused with data security, the discipline of protecting data from unauthorized parties.

Exam Probability: **High**

1. *Answer choices:*

(see index for correct answer)

- a. Data integrity
- b. Westi
- c. Thomas write rule
- d. Timestamp-based concurrency control

Guidance: level 1

:: Transport layer protocols ::

In computer networking, the _____ is a conceptual division of methods in the layered architecture of protocols in the network stack in the Internet protocol suite and the OSI model. The protocols of this layer provide host-to-host communication services for applications. It provides services such as connection-oriented communication, reliability, flow control, and multiplexing.

Exam Probability: **Medium**

2. *Answer choices:*

(see index for correct answer)

- a. Wireless transaction protocol
- b. Transport layer
- c. Licklider Transmission Protocol
- d. User Datagram Protocol

Guidance: level 1

:: HTML ::

_____ , or DHTML, is an umbrella term for a collection of technologies used together to create interactive and animated websites by using a combination of a static markup language , a client-side scripting language , a presentation definition language , and the Document Object Model . The application of DHTML was introduced by Microsoft with the release of Internet Explorer 4 in 1997.

Exam Probability: **High**

3. *Answer choices:*

(see index for correct answer)

- a. Dynamic HTML
- b. RDDL
- c. Link relation
- d. HTML attribute

Guidance: level 1

:: Windowing systems ::

_____ or MGR was an early windowing system originally designed and developed for Sun computers in 1984 by Stephen A. Uhler, then at Bellcore.

Exam Probability: **Low**

4. *Answer choices:*

(see index for correct answer)

- a. NeWS
- b. Windowing system
- c. ManaGeR
- d. WindowBlinds

Guidance: level 1

:: Unix programming tools ::

_____ is the magnitude or dimensions of a thing. _____ can be measured as length, width, height, diameter, perimeter, area, volume, or mass.

Exam Probability: **Low**

5. *Answer choices:*

(see index for correct answer)

- a. Hoc
- b. FASM
- c. Size
- d. Ktrace

Guidance: level 1

:: Analysis ::

_____ is the process of breaking a complex topic or substance into smaller parts in order to gain a better understanding of it. The technique has been applied in the study of mathematics and logic since before Aristotle, though _____ as a formal concept is a relatively recent development.

Exam Probability: **Medium**

6. *Answer choices:*

(see index for correct answer)

- a. Analytical quality control
- b. Situational analysis
- c. EATPUT
- d. Analysis

Guidance: level 1

:: Debuggers ::

_____ is the process of finding and resolving defects or problems within a computer program that prevent correct operation of computer software or a system.

Exam Probability: **High**

7. *Answer choices:*

(see index for correct answer)

- a. JSwat
- b. GNU Debugger
- c. Padre
- d. Jasik debugger

Guidance: level 1

:: Computer network security ::

A _____ is an application which controls network traffic to and from a computer, permitting or denying communications based on a security policy. Typically it works as an application layer firewall.

Exam Probability: **Low**

8. *Answer choices:*

(see index for correct answer)

- a. Personal firewall
- b. Google Safe Browsing
- c. Shell shoveling
- d. Port forwarding

Guidance: level 1

:: Operating systems ::

An _____ is system software that manages computer hardware and software resources and provides common services for computer programs.

Exam Probability: **Low**

9. *Answer choices:*

(see index for correct answer)

- a. LIO Target
- b. Supercomputer operating systems
- c. Data Access in Real Time
- d. Operating system

Guidance: level 1

:: Computing input devices ::

A _____ or smart pen is an input device which captures the handwriting or brush strokes of a user and converts handwritten analog information created using "pen and paper" into digital data, enabling the data to be utilized in various applications. This type of pen is usually used in conjunction with a digital notebook, although the data can also be used for different applications or simply as a graphic.

Exam Probability: **High**

10. *Answer choices:*

(see index for correct answer)

- a. Digital pen
- b. Videotelephony

- c. Finger tracking
- d. Logitech G27

Guidance: level 1

:: Software development ::

_____ is the process of conceiving, specifying, designing, programming, documenting, testing, and bug fixing involved in creating and maintaining applications, frameworks, or other software components. _____ is a process of writing and maintaining the source code, but in a broader sense, it includes all that is involved between the conception of the desired software through to the final manifestation of the software, sometimes in a planned and structured process. Therefore, _____ may include research, new development, prototyping, modification, reuse, re-engineering, maintenance, or any other activities that result in software products.

Exam Probability: **Medium**

11. *Answer choices:*
(see index for correct answer)

- a. Multi-channel app development
- b. Classification Tree Method
- c. Akka
- d. Software development

Guidance: level 1

:: Wireless networking ::

A _____ is a computer network that uses wireless data connections between network nodes.

Exam Probability: **High**

12. *Answer choices:*

(see index for correct answer)

- a. High-capacity data radio
- b. Silver Spring Networks
- c. Wireless Washtenaw
- d. Wireless site survey

Guidance: level 1

:: Knowledge representation ::

In general usage, a _____ is a reference work that lists words grouped together according to similarity of meaning , in contrast to a dictionary, which provides definitions for words, and generally lists them in alphabetical order. The main purpose of such reference works for users "to find the word, or words, by which [an] idea may be most fitly and aptly expressed," quoting Peter Mark Roget, author of Roget's _____ .

Exam Probability: **High**

13. *Answer choices:*

(see index for correct answer)

- a. Thesaurus
- b. Default logic
- c. Enaction
- d. Qualification problem

Guidance: level 1

:: Client-server database management systems ::

_____ is an open-source relational database management system. Its name is a combination of "My", the name of co-founder Michael Widenius's daughter, and "SQL", the abbreviation for Structured Query Language.

Exam Probability: **High**

14. *Answer choices:*

(see index for correct answer)

- a. MySQL
- b. Transbase
- c. PostgreSQL

Guidance: level 1

:: Files ::

A _____ in computers is a critical computer file without which a computer system may not operate correctly. These files may come as part of the operating system, a third-party device driver or other sources. Microsoft Windows and MS-DOS mark their more valuable _____ s with a "system" attribute to protect them against accidental deletion.

Exam Probability: **High**

15. *Answer choices:*

(see index for correct answer)

- a. System file
- b. Sparse file
- c. README
- d. JHOVE

Guidance: level 1

:: Audio storage ::

_____ is a digital optical disc data storage format that was co-developed by Philips and Sony and released in 1982. The format was originally developed to store and play only sound recordings but was later adapted for storage of data. Several other formats were further derived from these, including write-once audio and data storage, rewritable media, Video _____, Super Video _____, Photo CD, PictureCD, CD-i, and Enhanced Music CD. The first commercially available audio CD player, the Sony CDP-101, was released October 1982 in Japan.

Exam Probability: **High**

16. *Answer choices:*

(see index for correct answer)

- a. Oxide side
- b. Compact disc
- c. Vinyl record
- d. Record collecting

Guidance: level 1

:: Computing input devices ::

A _____ is a pointing device consisting of a ball held by a socket containing sensors to detect a rotation of the ball about two axes—like an upside-down mouse with an exposed protruding ball. The user rolls the ball to position the on-screen pointer, using their thumb, fingers, or commonly the palm of the hand while using the fingertips to press the mouse buttons.

Exam Probability: **Medium**

17. *Answer choices:*

(see index for correct answer)

- a. Trackball
- b. Paddle
- c. Samples per inch
- d. Finger tracking

Guidance: level 1

:: Graphical user interface elements ::

In computer interface design, a _____ is a graphical control element on which on-screen buttons, icons, menus, or other input or output elements are placed. _____ s are seen in many types of software such as office suites, graphics editors and web browsers. _____ s are usually distinguished from palettes by their integration into the edges of the screen or larger windows, which results in wasted space if too many underpopulated bars are stacked atop each other or interface inefficiency if overloaded bars are placed on small windows.

Exam Probability: **Low**

18. *Answer choices:*

(see index for correct answer)

- a. Toolbar
- b. Integration tree
- c. Menu
- d. Marching ants

Guidance: level 1

:: Virtual reality ::

_____ is an experience taking place within simulated and immersive environments that can be similar to or completely different from the real world. Applications of _____ can include entertainment and educational purposes. Other, distinct types of VR style technology include augmented reality and mixed reality.

Exam Probability: **High**

19. *Answer choices:*

(see index for correct answer)

- a. Eon Reality
- b. AGX Multiphysics
- c. Char Davies
- d. 3DML

Guidance: level 1

:: Physical layer protocols ::

In telecommunications and computer networks, _____ is a method by which multiple analog or digital signals are combined into one signal over a shared medium. The aim is to share a scarce resource. For example, in telecommunications, several telephone calls may be carried using one wire. _____ originated in telegraphy in the 1870s, and is now widely applied in communications. In telephony, George Owen Squier is credited with the development of telephone carrier _____ in 1910.

Exam Probability: **High**

20. *Answer choices:*

(see index for correct answer)

- a. Multiplexing
- b. Asynchronous serial communication
- c. Synchronous Serial Interface
- d. LocalTalk-to-Ethernet bridge

Guidance: level 1

:: Database management systems ::

A _____ or pillar in architecture and structural engineering is a structural element that transmits, through compression, the weight of the structure above to other structural elements below. In other words, a _____ is a compression member. The term _____ applies especially to a large round support with a capital and a base or pedestal which is made of stone, or appearing to be so. A small wooden or metal support is typically called a post, and supports with a rectangular or other non-round section are usually called piers. For the purpose of wind or earthquake engineering, _____ s may be designed to resist lateral forces. Other compression members are often termed " _____ s" because of the similar stress conditions. _____ s are frequently used to support beams or arches on which the upper parts of walls or ceilings rest. In architecture, " _____ " refers to such a structural element that also has certain proportional and decorative features. A _____ might also be a decorative element not needed for structural purposes; many _____ s are "engaged", that is to say form part of a wall.

Exam Probability: **Low**

21. *Answer choices:*

(see index for correct answer)

- a. Oracle Database
- b. Object Exchange Model
- c. Unique key
- d. AutoNumber

Guidance: level 1

:: Integrated development environments ::

_____ is a third-generation event-driven programming language from Microsoft for its Component Object Model programming model first released in 1991 and declared legacy during 2008. Microsoft intended _____ to be relatively easy to learn and use. _____ was derived from BASIC and enables the rapid application development of graphical user interface applications, access to databases using Data Access Objects, Remote Data Objects, or ActiveX Data Objects, and creation of ActiveX controls and objects.

Exam Probability: **Medium**

22. *Answer choices:*

(see index for correct answer)

- a. Hollywood
- b. IBM Rational Application Developer
- c. Visual Basic
- d. QuickC

Guidance: level 1

:: Cryptography ::

_____ or cryptology is the practice and study of techniques for secure communication in the presence of third parties called adversaries. More generally, _____ is about constructing and analyzing protocols that prevent third parties or the public from reading private messages; various aspects in information security such as data confidentiality, data integrity, authentication, and non-repudiation are central to modern _____. Modern _____ exists at the intersection of the disciplines of mathematics, computer science, electrical engineering, communication science, and physics. Applications of _____ include electronic commerce, chip-based payment cards, digital currencies, computer passwords, and military communications.

Exam Probability: **High**

23. *Answer choices:*

(see index for correct answer)

- a. Frederick Edward Hulme
- b. Proxy re-encryption
- c. CryptoParty
- d. Trusted Computing

Guidance: level 1

:: Computer access control ::

_____ is the act of confirming the truth of an attribute of a single piece of data claimed true by an entity. In contrast with identification, which refers to the act of stating or otherwise indicating a claim purportedly attesting to a person or thing's identity, _____ is the process of actually confirming that identity. It might involve confirming the identity of a person by validating their identity documents, verifying the authenticity of a website with a digital certificate, determining the age of an artifact by carbon dating, or ensuring that a product is what its packaging and labeling claim to be. In other words, _____ often involves verifying the validity of at least one form of identification.

Exam Probability: **Low**

24. *Answer choices:*

(see index for correct answer)

- a. Authentication
- b. Computational trust
- c. Google Authenticator
- d. Spring Security

Guidance: level 1

:: Computing output devices ::

An _____ is any piece of computer hardware equipment which converts information into human-readable form.

Exam Probability: **Medium**

25. *Answer choices:*

(see index for correct answer)

- a. GammaFax
- b. Output device
- c. Powerwall
- d. Palette

Guidance: level 1

:: Computer memory ::

_____ , in contrast to non-_____ , is computer memory that requires power to maintain the stored information; it retains its contents while powered on but when the power is interrupted, the stored data is quickly lost.

Exam Probability: **Medium**

26. *Answer choices:*

(see index for correct answer)

- a. Quad Data Rate SRAM
- b. External memory interface
- c. Content Addressable Parallel Processor
- d. Volatile memory

Guidance: level 1

:: Computer networking ::

A _____ or home area network is a type of computer network that facilitates communication among devices within the close vicinity of a home. Devices capable of participating in this network, for example, smart devices such as network printers and handheld mobile computers, often gain enhanced emergent capabilities through their ability to interact. These additional capabilities can be used to increase the quality of life inside the home in a variety of ways, such as automation of repetitive tasks, increased personal productivity, enhanced home security, and easier access to entertainment.

Exam Probability: **Low**

27. *Answer choices:*

(see index for correct answer)

- a. Fabric computing
- b. Versit Consortium
- c. Consolidation ratio
- d. Home network

Guidance: level 1

:: Computer buses ::

In computing, the _____ , expansion board, adapter card or accessory card is a printed circuit board that can be inserted into an electrical connector, or expansion slot, on a computer motherboard, backplane or riser card to add functionality to a computer system via the expansion bus.

Exam Probability: **Medium**

28. *Answer choices:*

(see index for correct answer)

- a. Multidrop bus
- b. Extended Industry Standard Architecture
- c. Expansion card
- d. Universal Graphics Module

Guidance: level 1

:: Fault-tolerant computer systems ::

Transaction processing is information processing in computer science that is divided into individual, indivisible operations called transactions. Each transaction must succeed or fail as a complete unit; it can never be only partially complete.

Exam Probability: **Medium**

29. *Answer choices:*

(see index for correct answer)

- a. Data synchronization
- b. Transaction processing
- c. Spanning Tree Protocol
- d. Processor array

Guidance: level 1

:: Java libraries ::

In computing, an _____ is any small application that performs one specific task that runs within the scope of a dedicated widget engine or a larger program, often as a plug-in. The term is frequently used to refer to a Java _____ , a program written in the Java programming language that is designed to be placed on a web page. _____ s are typical examples of transient and auxiliary applications that don't monopolize the user's attention. _____ s are not full-featured application programs, and are intended to be easily accessible.

Exam Probability: **Medium**

30. *Answer choices:*

(see index for correct answer)

- a. Javassist
- b. Commons Daemon
- c. Applet

- d. Java OpenAL

Guidance: level 1

:: Graphics file formats ::

_____ is a commonly used method of lossy compression for digital images, particularly for those images produced by digital photography. The degree of compression can be adjusted, allowing a selectable tradeoff between storage size and image quality. _____ typically achieves 10:1 compression with little perceptible loss in image quality.

Exam Probability: **High**

31. *Answer choices:*

(see index for correct answer)

- a. ICER
- b. BMP file format
- c. Truevision TGA
- d. JPEG

Guidance: level 1

:: Mereology ::

_____, in the abstract, is what belongs to or with something, whether as an attribute or as a component of said thing. In the context of this article, it is one or more components , whether physical or incorporeal, of a person's estate; or so belonging to, as in being owned by, a person or jointly a group of people or a legal entity like a corporation or even a society. Depending on the nature of the _____ , an owner of _____ has the right to consume, alter, share, redefine, rent, mortgage, pawn, sell, exchange, transfer, give away or destroy it, or to exclude others from doing these things, as well as to perhaps abandon it; whereas regardless of the nature of the _____ , the owner thereof has the right to properly use it , or at the very least exclusively keep it.

Exam Probability: **Low**

32. *Answer choices:*

(see index for correct answer)

- a. Property
- b. Mereological nihilism
- c. Non-wellfounded mereology
- d. Meronomy

Guidance: level 1

:: Computers ::

A _____ is a machine that can be instructed to carry out sequences of arithmetic or logical operations automatically via _____ programming. Modern _____ s have the ability to follow generalized sets of operations, called programs. These programs enable _____ s to perform an extremely wide range of tasks. A "complete" _____ including the hardware, the operating system , and peripheral equipment required and used for "full" operation can be referred to as a _____ system. This term may as well be used for a group of _____ s that are connected and work together, in particular a _____ network or _____ cluster.

Exam Probability: **High**

33. *Answer choices:*

(see index for correct answer)

- a. Cognitive computer
- b. Computer insurance
- c. Computer
- d. Lenovo Erazer X700

Guidance: level 1

:: Network architecture ::

_____ is the design of a computer network. It is a framework for the specification of a network's physical components and their functional organization and configuration, its operational principles and procedures, as well as communication protocols used.

Exam Probability: **Low**

34. *Answer choices:*

(see index for correct answer)

- a. Delay-tolerant networking
- b. Network architecture
- c. Gossip protocol
- d. Core-based trees

Guidance: level 1

:: Data management ::

_____ is an object-oriented program and library developed by CERN. It was originally designed for particle physics data analysis and contains several features specific to this field, but it is also used in other applications such as astronomy and data mining. The latest release is 6.16.00, as of 2018-11-14.

Exam Probability: **Medium**

35. *Answer choices:*

(see index for correct answer)

- a. Database schema
- b. NoCDN
- c. Data stream management system

- d. ROOT

Guidance: level 1

:: Computing input devices ::

A _____ is a computer input device that enables a user to hand-draw images, animations and graphics, with a special pen-like stylus, similar to the way a person draws images with a pencil and paper. These tablets may also be used to capture data or handwritten signatures. It can also be used to trace an image from a piece of paper which is taped or otherwise secured to the tablet surface. Capturing data in this way, by tracing or entering the corners of linear poly-lines or shapes, is called digitizing.

Exam Probability: **Medium**

36. *Answer choices:*

(see index for correct answer)

- a. Sign language glove
- b. Graphics tablet
- c. Smart Board
- d. Graffiti 2

Guidance: level 1

:: Programming language implementation ::

In computing, a _____ is an emulation of a computer system. _____ s are based on computer architectures and provide functionality of a physical computer. Their implementations may involve specialized hardware, software, or a combination.

Exam Probability: **Low**

37. *Answer choices:*

(see index for correct answer)

- a. Aspect weaver
- b. Conditional compilation
- c. Translator
- d. Virtual machine

Guidance: level 1

:: Information science ::

A _____ is a written, drawn, presented, or memorialized representation of thought. a _____ is a form, or written piece that trains a line of thought or as in history, a significant event. The word originates from the Latin _____ um, which denotes a "teaching" or "lesson": the verb doceo denotes "to teach". In the past, the word was usually used to denote a written proof useful as evidence of a truth or fact. In the computer age, " _____ " usually denotes a primarily textual computer file, including its structure and format, e.g. fonts, colors, and images. Contemporarily, " _____ " is not defined by its transmission medium, e.g., paper, given the existence of electronic _____ s. " _____ ation" is distinct because it has more denotations than " _____ ". _____ s are also distinguished from "realia", which are three-dimensional objects that would otherwise satisfy the definition of " _____ " because they memorialize or represent thought; _____ s are considered more as 2 dimensional representations. While _____ s are able to have large varieties of customization, all _____ s are able to be shared freely, and have the right to do so, creativity can be represented by _____ s, also. History, events, examples, opinion, etc. all can be expressed in _____ s.

Exam Probability: **High**

38. *Answer choices:*

(see index for correct answer)

- a. Overcategorization
- b. Paperless society
- c. Digital South Asia Library
- d. Document

Guidance: level 1

:: Graphical user interface elements ::

The _____ is a graphical control element in the form of a small window that communicates information to the user and prompts them for a response.

Exam Probability: **High**

39. *Answer choices:*
(see index for correct answer)

- a. Soft key
- b. GroupBar
- c. Dialog box
- d. Loading screen

Guidance: level 1

:: Network management ::

A _____ is the person designated in an organization whose responsibility includes maintaining computer infrastructures with emphasis on networking. Responsibilities may vary between organizations, but on-site servers, software-network interactions as well as network integrity/resilience are the key areas of focus.

Exam Probability: **Low**

40. *Answer choices:*

(see index for correct answer)

- a. Network element
- b. HP OpenView
- c. Desktop Management Interface
- d. Network Load Balancing Services

Guidance: level 1

:: Photo software ::

_____ is a raster graphics editor developed and published by Adobe Inc. for Windows and macOS. It was originally created in 1988 by Thomas and John Knoll. Since then, this software has become the industry standard not only in raster graphics editing, but in digital art as a whole. The software's name has thus become a generic trademark, leading to its usage as a verb although Adobe discourages such use. Photoshop can edit and compose raster images in multiple layers and supports masks, alpha compositing, and several color models including RGB, CMYK, CIELAB, spot color, and duotone. Photoshop uses its own <code>PSD</code> and <code>PSB</code> file formats to support these features. In addition to raster graphics, this software has limited abilities to edit or render text and vector graphics , as well as 3D graphics and video. Its feature set can be expanded by plug-ins; programs developed and distributed independently of Photoshop that run inside it and offer new or enhanced features.

Exam Probability: **Medium**

41. *Answer choices:*

(see index for correct answer)

- a. Noise Ninja
- b. Flash Gallery
- c. Portrait Professional
- d. Adobe Photoshop

Guidance: level 1

:: Local area networks ::

A _____ is a computer network that interconnects computers within a limited area such as a residence, school, laboratory, university campus or office building. By contrast, a wide area network not only covers a larger geographic distance, but also generally involves leased telecommunication circuits.

Exam Probability: **High**

42. *Answer choices:*

(see index for correct answer)

- a. Local area network
- b. Subinterface
- c. Ethernet over copper
- d. IBM PC Network

Guidance: level 1

:: Programming paradigms ::

_____ is a programming paradigm based on the concept of "objects", which can contain data, in the form of fields, and code, in the form of procedures. A feature of objects is an object's procedures that can access and often modify the data fields of the object with which they are associated. In OOP, computer programs are designed by making them out of objects that interact with one another. OOP languages are diverse, but the most popular ones are class-based, meaning that objects are instances of classes, which also determine their types.

Exam Probability: **Low**

43. *Answer choices:*

(see index for correct answer)

- a. Declarative programming
- b. Object-oriented programming

Guidance: level 1

:: Hypertext ::

_____ is text displayed on a computer display or other electronic devices with references to other text that the reader can immediately access. _____ documents are interconnected by hyperlinks, which are typically activated by a mouse click, keypress set or by touching the screen. Apart from text, the term " _____ " is also sometimes used to describe tables, images, and other presentational content formats with integrated hyperlinks. _____ is one of the key underlying concepts of the World Wide Web, where Web pages are often written in the _____ Markup Language . As implemented on the Web, _____ enables the easy-to-use publication of information over the Internet.

Exam Probability: **Low**

44. *Answer choices:*
(see index for correct answer)

- a. HyperCard
- b. Inline linking
- c. Object hyperlinking
- d. Hypertext

Guidance: level 1

:: Computer file systems ::

In computing, _____ code or an _____ file or _____ program, sometimes simply referred to as an _____ , causes a computer "to perform indicated tasks according to encoded instructions", as opposed to a data file that must be parsed by a program to be meaningful.

Exam Probability: **Low**

45. *Answer choices:*

(see index for correct answer)

- a. Installable File System
- b. Next3
- c. EFI System partition
- d. Executable

Guidance: level 1

:: Top-level domains ::

A _____ is one of the domains at the highest level in the hierarchical Domain Name System of the Internet. The _____ names are installed in the root zone of the name space. For all domains in lower levels, it is the last part of the domain name, that is, the last label of a fully qualified domain name. For example, in the domain name www.example.com, the _____ is com. Responsibility for management of most _____ s is delegated to specific organizations by the Internet Corporation for Assigned Names and Numbers , which operates the Internet Assigned Numbers Authority , and is in charge of maintaining the DNS root zone.

Exam Probability: **High**

46. *Answer choices:*

(see index for correct answer)

- a. Generic top-level domain
- b. Top-level domain
- c. Agency for the Development of the Information Society
- d. Internationalized country code top-level domain

Guidance: level 1

:: Artificial intelligence ::

In computer science, _____ , sometimes called machine intelligence, is intelligence demonstrated by machines, in contrast to the natural intelligence displayed by humans and animals. Colloquially, the term "_____" is used to describe machines that mimic "cognitive" functions that humans associate with other human minds, such as "learning" and "problem solving".

Exam Probability: **High**

47. *Answer choices:*

(see index for correct answer)

- a. GOFAI
- b. Intelligent despatch
- c. Artificial intelligence
- d. Action selection

Guidance: level 1

:: Malware ::

The _____ is a story from the Trojan War about the subterfuge that the Greeks used to enter the independent city of Troy and win the war. In the canonical version, after a fruitless 10-year siege, the Greeks constructed a huge wooden horse, and hid a select force of men inside including Odysseus. The Greeks pretended to sail away, and the Trojans pulled the horse into their city as a victory trophy. That night the Greek force crept out of the horse and opened the gates for the rest of the Greek army, which had sailed back under cover of night. The Greeks entered and destroyed the city of Troy, ending the war.

Exam Probability: **High**

48. *Answer choices:*
(see index for correct answer)

- a. Power virus
- b. Trojan horse
- c. Micro Bill Systems
- d. Network Crack Program Hacker Group

Guidance: level 1

:: Computer access control ::

A _____ is a user of a website, program, or other system who has previously registered. _____ s normally provide some sort of credentials to the system in order to prove their identity: this is known as logging in. Systems intended for use by the general public often allow any user to register simply by selecting a register or sign up function and providing these credentials for the first time. _____ s may be granted privileges beyond those granted to un _____ s.

Exam Probability: **Low**

49. *Answer choices:*

(see index for correct answer)

- a. PassWindow
- b. Registered user
- c. Pre-boot authentication
- d. Java Authentication and Authorization Service

Guidance: level 1

:: History of the Internet ::

The _____ is a standard network protocol used for the transfer of computer files between a client and server on a computer network.

Exam Probability: **High**

50. *Answer choices:*

(see index for correct answer)

- a. International Internet Preservation Consortium
- b. Montevideo Statement on the Future of Internet Cooperation
- c. North American Network Operators%27 Group
- d. File Transfer Protocol

Guidance: level 1

:: Virtual reality ::

The _____ is the global system of interconnected computer networks that use the _____ protocol suite to link devices worldwide. It is a network of networks that consists of private, public, academic, business, and government networks of local to global scope, linked by a broad array of electronic, wireless, and optical networking technologies. The _____ carries a vast range of information resources and services, such as the inter-linked hypertext documents and applications of the World Wide Web, electronic mail, telephony, and file sharing.

Exam Probability: **Medium**

51. *Answer choices:*

(see index for correct answer)

- a. Unreal Engine
- b. Internet

- c. 3D user interaction
- d. OpenGL

Guidance: level 1

:: Software architecture ::

The _____ is a form of user interface that allows users to interact with electronic devices through graphical icons and visual indicators such as secondary notation, instead of text-based user interfaces, typed command labels or text navigation. GUIs were introduced in reaction to the perceived steep learning curve of command-line interfaces , which require commands to be typed on a computer keyboard.

Exam Probability: **Low**

52. *Answer choices:*

(see index for correct answer)

- a. Presentation logic
- b. Library Oriented Architecture
- c. Connascence
- d. Graphical user interface

Guidance: level 1

:: Computer memory ::

In computing, a _____ is a printed circuit board on which memory integrated circuits are mounted. _____ s permit easy installation and replacement in electronic systems, especially computers such as personal computers, workstations, and servers. The first _____ s were proprietary designs that were specific to a model of computer from a specific manufacturer. Later, _____ s were standardized by organizations such as JEDEC and could be used in any system designed to use them.

Exam Probability: **High**

53. *Answer choices:*

(see index for correct answer)

- a. CAS latency
- b. Memory bank
- c. Memory module
- d. Base address

Guidance: level 1

:: Software requirements ::

In product development and process optimization, a _____ is a singular documented physical or functional need that a particular design, product or process aims to satisfy. It is commonly used in a formal sense in engineering design, including for example in systems engineering, software engineering, or enterprise engineering. It is a broad concept that could speak to any necessary function, attribute, capability, characteristic, or quality of a system for it to have value and utility to a customer, organization, internal user, or other stakeholder. _____ s can come with different levels of specificity; for example, a _____ specification or _____ "spec" refers to an explicit, highly objective/clear _____ to be satisfied by a material, design, product, or service.

Exam Probability: **Low**

54. *Answer choices:*

(see index for correct answer)

- a. Requirement
- b. Use Case Diagram
- c. Requirements Modeling Framework
- d. Soft goal

Guidance: level 1

:: Holism ::

_____ characterises the behaviour of a system or model whose components interact in multiple ways and follow local rules, meaning there is no reasonable higher instruction to define the various possible interactions.

Exam Probability: **Medium**

55. *Answer choices:*

(see index for correct answer)

- a. Confirmation holism
- b. Complementary holism
- c. Integral ecology
- d. Antireductionism

Guidance: level 1

:: Control characters ::

_____ is the boundless three-dimensional extent in which objects and events have relative position and direction. Physical _____ is often conceived in three linear dimensions, although modern physicists usually consider it, with time, to be part of a boundless four-dimensional continuum known as _____ time. The concept of _____ is considered to be of fundamental importance to an understanding of the physical universe. However, disagreement continues between philosophers over whether it is itself an entity, a relationship between entities, or part of a conceptual framework.

Exam Probability: **Medium**

56. *Answer choices:*

(see index for correct answer)

- a. Carriage return
- b. Space
- c. Line starve
- d. Zero-width non-joiner

Guidance: level 1

:: Computing input devices ::

In computing, an _____ is a piece of computer hardware equipment used to provide data and control signals to an information processing system such as a computer or information appliance. Examples of _____ s include keyboards, mouse, scanners, digital cameras and joysticks. Audio _____ s may be used for purposes including speech recognition. Many companies are utilizing speech recognition to help assist users to use their device.

Exam Probability: **High**

57. *Answer choices:*
(see index for correct answer)

- a. Point-and-shoot interface
- b. Input device
- c. Text entry interface
- d. Sensorium Project

Guidance: level 1

:: Business software ::

_____ is application software used for producing information. Its names arose from the fact that it increases productivity, especially of individual office workers, from typists to knowledge workers, although its scope is now wider than that. Office suites, which brought word processing, spreadsheet, and relational database programs to the desktop in the 1980s, are the core example of _____. They revolutionized the office with the magnitude of the productivity increase they brought as compared with the pre-1980s office environments of typewriters, paper filing, and handwritten lists and ledgers. In the United States, some 78% of "middle-skill" occupations now require the use of _____. In the 2010s, _____ has become even more consumerized than it already was, as computing becomes ever more integrated into daily personal life.

Exam Probability: **Low**

58. *Answer choices:*
(see index for correct answer)

- a. Productivity software
- b. Clubscan
- c. Xpert-Timer
- d. Very Large Business Applications

Guidance: level 1

:: Infographics ::

A _____ is a symbolic representation of information according to visualization technique. _____ s have been used since ancient times, but became more prevalent during the Enlightenment. Sometimes, the technique uses a three-dimensional visualization which is then projected onto a two-dimensional surface. The word graph is sometimes used as a synonym for _____ .

Exam Probability: **High**

59. *Answer choices:*

(see index for correct answer)

- a. DOT pictograms
- b. MaSSHandra
- c. Planimetrics
- d. Check sheet

Guidance: level 1

Computers

A computer is a device that can be instructed to carry out sequences of arithmetic or logical operations automatically via computer programming. Modern computers have the ability to follow generalized sets of operations, called programs. These programs enable computers to perform an extremely wide range of tasks.

:: Codecs ::

_____ is the process of converting an analog video signal—such as that produced by a video camera, DVD player, or television tuner—to digital video and sending it to local storage or to external circuitry. The resulting digital data are referred to as a digital video stream, or more often, simply video stream. Depending on the application, a video stream may be recorded as computer files, or sent to a video display, or both.

Exam Probability: **Medium**

1. *Answer choices:*

(see index for correct answer)

- a. Windows Media Components for QuickTime
- b. Tieline
- c. Video capture
- d. Combined Community Codec Pack

Guidance: level 1

:: Digital typography ::

_____ is a page description language in the electronic publishing and desktop publishing business. It is a dynamically typed, concatenative programming language and was created at Adobe Systems by John Warnock, Charles Geschke, Doug Brotz, Ed Taft and Bill Paxton from 1982 to 1984.

Exam Probability: **Medium**

2. *Answer choices:*

(see index for correct answer)

- a. TeX font metric
- b. Core fonts for the Web
- c. Vector font
- d. Fill character

Guidance: level 1

:: Central processing unit ::

A _____ or modified bit is a bit that is associated with a block of computer memory and indicates whether or not the corresponding block of memory has been modified. The _____ is set when the processor writes to this memory. The bit indicates that its associated block of memory has been modified and has not been saved to storage yet. When a block of memory is to be replaced, its corresponding _____ is checked to see if the block needs to be written back to secondary memory before being replaced or if it can simply be removed. _____ s are used by the CPU cache and in the page replacement algorithms of an operating system.

Exam Probability: **High**

3. *Answer choices:*

(see index for correct answer)

- a. Super-threading
- b. Dirty bit
- c. Scalar processor
- d. Bit slicing

Guidance: level 1

:: Computer data ::

In computer science, _____ is the ability to access an arbitrary element of a sequence in equal time or any datum from a population of addressable elements roughly as easily and efficiently as any other, no matter how many elements may be in the set. It is typically contrasted to sequential access.

Exam Probability: **Medium**

4. *Answer choices:*

(see index for correct answer)

- a. Data at Rest
- b. 12-bit
- c. Hex editor
- d. Data efficiency

Guidance: level 1

:: Healthcare software ::

The Veterans Information Systems and Technology Architecture is the nationwide veterans clinical and business information system of the U.S. Department of Veterans Affairs. _____ consists of 180 applications for clinical, financial, and administrative functions all integrated within a single database, providing single, authoritative source of data for all veteran-related care and services. The U.S. Congress mandates the VA keep the veterans health record in a single, authoritative, lifelong database, which is _____.

Exam Probability: **Low**

5. *Answer choices:*

(see index for correct answer)

- a. Ubuntu-Med
- b. CommonGround
- c. VistA
- d. Composite Health Care System

Guidance: level 1

:: Network addressing ::

An Internet Protocol address is a numerical label assigned to each device connected to a computer network that uses the Internet Protocol for communication. An _____ serves two principal functions: host or network interface identification and location addressing.

Exam Probability: **Low**

6. *Answer choices:*

(see index for correct answer)

- a. Dot-decimal notation
- b. Multicast address
- c. Virtual IP address

- d. IP address

Guidance: level 1

:: Machine code ::

In computing, an _____ is the portion of a machine language instruction that specifies the operation to be performed. Beside the _____ itself, most instructions also specify the data they will process, in the form of operands. In addition to _____ s used in the instruction set architectures of various CPUs, which are hardware devices, they can also be used in abstract computing machines as part of their byte code specifications.

Exam Probability: **Low**

7. *Answer choices:*

(see index for correct answer)

- a. Indirect branch
- b. Object code
- c. Machine code
- d. Operand

Guidance: level 1

:: Network architecture ::

An _____ is a type of optical telecommunications network employing wired fiber-optic communication or wireless free-space optical communication in a mesh network architecture.

Exam Probability: **Medium**

8. *Answer choices:*
_(see index for correct answer)

- a. Context aware network
- b. Segment protection
- c. Split multi-link trunking
- d. Distributed Multi-Link Trunking

Guidance: level 1

:: Computer memory form factor ::

A _____ , or single in-line memory module, is a type of memory module containing random-access memory used in computers from the early 1980s to the late 1990s. It differs from a dual in-line memory module , the most predominant form of memory module today, in that the contacts on a _____ are redundant on both sides of the module. _____ s were standardised under the JEDEC JESD-21C standard.

Exam Probability: **Medium**

9. *Answer choices:*

(see index for correct answer)

- a. SO-DIMM
- b. SIMM

Guidance: level 1

:: Data structures ::

In computer science, a _____ is a data structure used by a language translator such as a compiler or interpreter, where each identifier in a program's source code is associated with information relating to its declaration or appearance in the source. _____ stores the information related about the symbol.

Exam Probability: **Medium**

10. *Answer choices:*

(see index for correct answer)

- a. Dynamization
- b. Process Environment Block
- c. Linked data structure
- d. Symbol table

Guidance: level 1

:: Compilers ::

A _____ is a computer program that translates computer code written in one programming language into another programming language. The name _____ is primarily used for programs that translate source code from a high-level programming language to a lower level language to create an executable program.

Exam Probability: **High**

11. *Answer choices:*

(see index for correct answer)

- a. Linkage
- b. Multi-pass compiler
- c. One-pass compiler
- d. Edison Design Group

Guidance: level 1

:: Error detection and correction ::

A _____, or check bit, is a bit added to a string of binary code to ensure that the total number of 1-bits in the string is even or odd. _____ s are used as the simplest form of error detecting code.

Exam Probability: **Low**

12. *Answer choices:*

(see index for correct answer)

- a. Repeat-accumulate code
- b. BCH code
- c. Residual bit error rate
- d. AN codes

Guidance: level 1

:: Educational programming languages ::

A _____ is a physiological capacity of organisms that provides data for perception. The _____ s and their operation, classification, and theory are overlapping topics studied by a variety of fields, most notably neuroscience, cognitive psychology, and philosophy of perception. The nervous system has a specific sensory nervous system, and a _____ organ, or sensor, dedicated to each _____ .

Exam Probability: **Medium**

13. *Answer choices:*

(see index for correct answer)

- a. IITRAN
- b. Sense

- c. UCBLogo
- d. Robic

Guidance: level 1

:: Digital television ::

In signal processing, _____ , source coding, or bit-rate reduction involves encoding information using fewer bits than the original representation. Compression can be either lossy or lossless. Lossless compression reduces bits by identifying and eliminating statistical redundancy. No information is lost in lossless compression. Lossy compression reduces bits by removing unnecessary or less important information.

Exam Probability: **Medium**

14. *Answer choices:*

(see index for correct answer)

- a. Televisi%C3%B3 Digital Terrestre
- b. Internet television
- c. Digea
- d. Data compression

Guidance: level 1

:: Internet architecture ::

_____ is defined as that aspect of Internet network engineering dealing with the issue of performance evaluation and performance optimization of operational IP networks. Traffic engineering encompasses the application of technology and scientific principles to the measurement, characterization, modeling, and control of Internet traffic [RFC-2702, AWD2].

Exam Probability: **Low**

15. *Answer choices:*

(see index for correct answer)

- a. Internet traffic engineering
- b. Routing table
- c. AS 7007 incident
- d. Network address translation

Guidance: level 1

:: Central processing unit ::

An _____ architecture is an abstract model of a computer. It is also referred to as architecture or computer architecture. A realization of an ISA is called an implementation. An ISA permits multiple implementations that may vary in performance, physical size, and monetary cost ; because the ISA serves as the interface between software and hardware. Software that has been written for an ISA can run on different implementations of the same ISA. This has enabled binary compatibility between different generations of computers to be easily achieved, and the development of computer families. Both of these developments have helped to lower the cost of computers and to increase their applicability. For these reasons, the ISA is one of the most important abstractions in computing today.

Exam Probability: **Medium**

16. *Answer choices:*

(see index for correct answer)

- a. Microcode
- b. Instruction set
- c. Stepping level
- d. Temporal multithreading

Guidance: level 1

:: Automatic identification and data capture ::

A bar code reader is an electronic device that can read and output printed barcodes to a computer. Like a flatbed scanner, it consists of a light source, a lens and a light sensor translating for optical impulses into electrical signals. Additionally, nearly all _____ s contain decoder circuitry analyzing the bar code's image data provided by the sensor and sending the barcode's content to the scanner's output port.

Exam Probability: **High**

17. *Answer choices:*

(see index for correct answer)

- a. Barcode reader
- b. High-frequency direction finding
- c. Radio-frequency identification
- d. Association for Automatic Identification and Mobility

Guidance: level 1

:: Interrupts ::

In computer systems programming, an _____ , also known as an interrupt service routine or ISR, is a special block of code associated with a specific interrupt condition. _____ s are initiated by hardware interrupts, software interrupt instructions, or software exceptions, and are used for implementing device drivers or transitions between protected modes of operation, such as system calls.

Exam Probability: **Medium**

18. *Answer choices:*

(see index for correct answer)

- a. Intel APIC Architecture
- b. Interrupt coalescing
- c. Interrupt flag
- d. Interrupt handler

Guidance: level 1

:: Review websites ::

A _____ is an evaluation of a publication, service, or company such as a movie, video game, musical composition, book; a piece of hardware like a car, home appliance, or computer; or an event or performance, such as a live music concert, play, musical theater show, dance show, or art exhibition. In addition to a critical evaluation, the _____'s author may assign the work a rating to indicate its relative merit. More loosely, an author may _____ current events, trends, or items in the news. A compilation of _____ s may itself be called a _____. The New York _____ of Books, for instance, is a collection of essays on literature, culture, and current affairs. National _____, founded by William F. Buckley, Jr., is an influential conservative magazine, and Monthly _____ is a long-running socialist periodical.

Exam Probability: **Low**

19. *Answer choices:*

(see index for correct answer)

- a. Kudzu.com
- b. Release Magazine
- c. Qype
- d. Review

Guidance: level 1

:: Central processing unit ::

A _____ is a collection of functional units such as arithmetic logic units or multipliers, that perform data processing operations, registers, and buses. Along with the control unit it composes the central processing unit .. A larger _____ can be made by joining more than one number of _____ s using multiplexer.

Exam Probability: **Low**

20. *Answer choices:*

(see index for correct answer)

- a. Stepping level
- b. Stack register
- c. Instruction set
- d. Datapath

Guidance: level 1

:: Computer architecture ::

The _____ —also known as the von Neumann model or Princeton architecture—is a computer architecture based on a 1945 description by the mathematician and physicist John von Neumann and others in the First Draft of a Report on the EDVAC. That document describes a design architecture for an electronic digital computer with these components.

Exam Probability: **Low**

21. *Answer choices:*

(see index for correct answer)

- a. Memory dependence prediction
- b. Vectored Interrupt
- c. Von Neumann architecture
- d. Anykernel

Guidance: level 1

:: Application layer protocols ::

An _____ is an abstraction layer that specifies the shared communications protocols and interface methods used by hosts in a communications network. The _____ abstraction is used in both of the standard models of computer networking: the Internet Protocol Suite and the OSI model. Although both models use the same term for their respective highest level layer, the detailed definitions and purposes are different.

Exam Probability: **Low**

22. *Answer choices:*

(see index for correct answer)

- a. Simple Network Management Protocol
- b. Mail Transfer Protocol
- c. Realtek Remote Control Protocol
- d. Application layer

Guidance: level 1

:: Mathematical logic ::

_____ is an arrangement and organization of interrelated elements in a material object or system, or the object or system so organized. Material _____ s include man-made objects such as buildings and machines and natural objects such as biological organisms, minerals and chemicals. Abstract _____ s include data _____ s in computer science and musical form. Types of _____ include a hierarchy, a network featuring many-to-many links, or a lattice featuring connections between components that are neighbors in space.

Exam Probability: **High**

23. *Answer choices:*

(see index for correct answer)

- a. Structure
- b. Algebraic definition
- c. Superposition calculus
- d. Predicate

Guidance: level 1

:: Network protocols ::

_____ is a standardized wide area network technology that specifies the physical and data link layers of digital telecommunications channels using a packet switching methodology. Originally designed for transport across Integrated Services Digital Network infrastructure, it may be used today in the context of many other network interfaces.

Exam Probability: **Low**

24. *Answer choices:*

(see index for correct answer)

- a. Virtual Link Aggregation Control Protocol
- b. NWLink

- c. Frame Relay
- d. Lantastic

Guidance: level 1

:: Instruction set architectures ::

_____ is a reduced instruction set computing instruction set architecture created by the 1991 Apple–IBM–Motorola alliance, known as AIM. _____ , as an evolving instruction set, has since 2006 been named Power ISA, while the old name lives on as a trademark for some implementations of Power Architecture-based processors.

Exam Probability: **Low**

25. *Answer choices:*

(see index for correct answer)

- a. PowerPC
- b. Itanium

Guidance: level 1

:: Polyhedra ::

A _____ is a piece of fabric with a distinctive design and colours. It is used as a symbol, a signalling device, or for decoration. The term _____ is also used to refer to the graphic design employed, and _____ s have evolved into a general tool for rudimentary signalling and identification, especially in environments where communication is challenging. The study of _____ s is known as "vexillology" from the Latin vexillum, meaning "_____" or "banner".

Exam Probability: **Low**

26. *Answer choices:*

(see index for correct answer)

- a. Small complex rhombicosidodecahedron
- b. Schwarz triangle
- c. Tetrahedrally diminished dodecahedron
- d. Flag

Guidance: level 1

:: Computer memory ::

In computing, a _____ is a reference to a specific memory location used at various levels by software and hardware. _____ es are fixed-length sequences of digits conventionally displayed and manipulated as unsigned integers. Such numerical semantic bases itself upon features of CPU, as well upon use of the memory like an array endorsed by various programming languages.

Exam Probability: **High**

27. *Answer choices:*

(see index for correct answer)

- a. Sigmaquad
- b. Read-only memory
- c. Drum memory
- d. CompactFlash

Guidance: level 1

:: Radio modulation modes ::

In telecommunications and signal processing, _____ is the encoding of information in a carrier wave by varying the instantaneous frequency of the wave.

Exam Probability: **Medium**

28. *Answer choices:*

(see index for correct answer)

- a. Slow-scan television
- b. Carrierless amplitude phase modulation
- c. Independent sideband
- d. Frequency modulation

Guidance: level 1

:: Data types ::

The _____ is a unit of digital information that most commonly consists of eight bits, representing a binary number. Historically, the _____ was the number of bits used to encode a single character of text in a computer and for this reason it is the smallest addressable unit of memory in many computer architectures.

Exam Probability: **Low**

29. *Answer choices:*

(see index for correct answer)

- a. Byte
- b. Complex data type
- c. Type conversion
- d. Subtyping

Guidance: level 1

:: Digital registers ::

In computing, the _____ or current _____ is the part of a CPU's control unit that holds the instruction currently being executed or decoded. In simple processors each instruction to be executed is loaded into the _____ which holds it while it is decoded, prepared and ultimately executed, which can take several steps.

Exam Probability: **Medium**

30. *Answer choices:*

(see index for correct answer)

- a. Device register
- b. Memory data register
- c. Dekatron
- d. Memory address register

Guidance: level 1

:: Digital registers ::

In a computer, the Memory Address Register is the CPU register that either stores the memory address from which data will be fetched from the CPU, or the address to which data will be sent and stored.

Exam Probability: **Medium**

31. *Answer choices:*

(see index for correct answer)

- a. Spill metric
- b. Memory address register
- c. Address-range register
- d. Interrupt control register

Guidance: level 1

:: Computing platforms ::

_____ is a family of open source Unix-like operating systems based on the _____ kernel, an operating system kernel first released on September 17, 1991 by Linus Torvalds. _____ is typically packaged in a _____ distribution .

Exam Probability: **Medium**

32. *Answer choices:*

(see index for correct answer)

- a. MINIX 3
- b. Java Platform, Enterprise Edition
- c. Genera
- d. Linux

Guidance: level 1

:: Network layer protocols ::

In the seven-layer OSI model of computer networking, the _____ is layer 3. The _____ is responsible for packet forwarding including routing through intermediate routers.

Exam Probability: **Medium**

33. *Answer choices:*
(see index for correct answer)

- a. ICMPv6
- b. Internet Group Management Protocol with Access Control
- c. Grapple
- d. Network Layer

Guidance: level 1

:: ARM architecture ::

An _____ is a sweet, edible fruit produced by an _____ tree. _____ trees are cultivated worldwide and are the most widely grown species in the genus Malus. The tree originated in Central Asia, where its wild ancestor, Malus sieversii, is still found today. _____ s have been grown for thousands of years in Asia and Europe and were brought to North America by European colonists. _____ s have religious and mythological significance in many cultures, including Norse, Greek and European Christian traditions.

Exam Probability: **Medium**

34. *Answer choices:*

(see index for correct answer)

- a. Apple
- b. Armhf
- c. Genesi
- d. ARM7

Guidance: level 1

:: Digital electronics ::

In digital circuit theory, _____ logic is a type of digital logic which is implemented by Boolean circuits, where the output is a pure function of the present input only. This is in contrast to sequential logic, in which the output depends not only on the present input but also on the history of the input. In other words, sequential logic has memory while _____ logic does not.

Exam Probability: **High**

35. *Answer choices:*

(see index for correct answer)

- a. Triggering device
- b. PLEDM
- c. Power network design
- d. Combinational

Guidance: level 1

:: Computer memory ::

_____ is a form of computer data storage that stores data and machine code currently being used. A _____ device allows data items to be read or written in almost the same amount of time irrespective of the physical location of data inside the memory. In contrast, with other direct-access data storage media such as hard disks, CD-RWs, DVD-RWs and the older magnetic tapes and drum memory, the time required to read and write data items varies significantly depending on their physical locations on the recording medium, due to mechanical limitations such as media rotation speeds and arm movement.

Exam Probability: **Low**

36. *Answer choices:*

(see index for correct answer)

- a. Thin-film memory
- b. Random-access memory
- c. Non-volatile random-access memory
- d. CompactFlash

Guidance: level 1

:: Central processing unit ::

In computing, a _____ or array processor is a central processing unit that implements an instruction set containing instructions that operate on one-dimensional arrays of data called vectors, compared to the scalar processors, whose instructions operate on single data items. _____ s can greatly improve performance on certain workloads, notably numerical simulation and similar tasks. Vector machines appeared in the early 1970s and dominated supercomputer design through the 1970s into the 1990s, notably the various Cray platforms. The rapid fall in the price-to-performance ratio of conventional microprocessor designs led to the vector supercomputer's demise in the later 1990s.

Exam Probability: **Low**

37. *Answer choices:*

(see index for correct answer)

- a. Ring
- b. Microsequencer
- c. Project Denver
- d. Vector processor

Guidance: level 1

:: Digital circuits ::

An _____ is a combinational digital electronic circuit that performs arithmetic and bitwise operations on integer binary numbers. This is in contrast to a floating-point unit, which operates on floating point numbers. An ALU is a fundamental building block of many types of computing circuits, including the central processing unit of computers, FPUs, and graphics processing units. A single CPU, FPU or GPU may contain multiple ALUs.

Exam Probability: **Low**

38. *Answer choices:*

(see index for correct answer)

- a. Arithmetic logic unit
- b. Wallace tree
- c. High impedance
- d. Decoder

Guidance: level 1

:: Data types ::

In computing, a _____ , is a memory address that is represented in the form of a binary number on the address bus circuitry in order to enable the data bus to access a particular storage cell of main memory, or a register of memory mapped I/O device.

Exam Probability: **High**

39. *Answer choices:*

(see index for correct answer)

- a. Boolean data type
- b. Minifloat
- c. Physical address
- d. Type conversion

Guidance: level 1

:: Logic gates ::

In digital electronics, a _____ is a logic gate which produces an output which is false only if all its inputs are true; thus its output is complement to that of an AND gate. A LOW output results only if all the inputs to the gate are HIGH ; if any input is LOW , a HIGH output results. A _____ is made using transistors and junction diodes. By De Morgan's theorem, a two-input _____ 's logic may be expressed as AB=A+B, making a _____ equivalent to inverters followed by an OR gate.

Exam Probability: **High**

40. *Answer choices:*

(see index for correct answer)

- a. xnor
- b. NAND gate
- c. xnor gate
- d. xor gate

Guidance: level 1

:: Instruction processing ::

The _____ is the cycle which the central processing unit follows from boot-up until the computer has shut down in order to process instructions. It is composed of three main stages: the fetch stage, the decode stage, and the execute stage.

Exam Probability: **High**

41. *Answer choices:*

(see index for correct answer)

- a. Instruction cycle
- b. WRMSR
- c. Memory barrier
- d. Bubble

Guidance: level 1

:: Computing input devices ::

In computing, an _____ is a piece of computer hardware equipment used to provide data and control signals to an information processing system such as a computer or information appliance. Examples of _____ s include keyboards, mouse, scanners, digital cameras and joysticks. Audio _____ s may be used for purposes including speech recognition. Many companies are utilizing speech recognition to help assist users to use their device.

Exam Probability: **Low**

42. *Answer choices:*

(see index for correct answer)

- a. Touchatag
- b. Orbita mouse
- c. Input device
- d. Camera module

Guidance: level 1

:: Infographics ::

A _____ is a type of diagram used in computer science and related fields to describe the behavior of systems. _____ s require that the system described is composed of a finite number of states; sometimes, this is indeed the case, while at other times this is a reasonable abstraction. Many forms of _____ s exist, which differ slightly and have different semantics.

Exam Probability: **Medium**

43. *Answer choices:*

(see index for correct answer)

- a. Archaeological plan
- b. Bumper sticker
- c. State diagram
- d. House sign

Guidance: level 1

:: Computer security software ::

In computer networks, a _____ is a server that acts as an intermediary for requests from clients seeking resources from other servers. A client connects to the _____, requesting some service, such as a file, connection, web page, or other resource available from a different server and the _____ evaluates the request as a way to simplify and control its complexity. Proxies were invented to add structure and encapsulation to distributed systems.

Exam Probability: **Low**

44. *Answer choices:*

(see index for correct answer)

- a. Norton AntiBot
- b. Proxy server
- c. Employee monitoring software
- d. Chkrootkit

Guidance: level 1

:: Computer architecture ::

The _____ is a computer architecture with physically separate storage and signal pathways for instructions and data. The term originated from the Harvard Mark I relay-based computer, which stored instructions on punched tape and data in electro-mechanical counters. These early machines had data storage entirely contained within the central processing unit, and provided no access to the instruction storage as data. Programs needed to be loaded by an operator; the processor could not initialize itself.

Exam Probability: **Medium**

45. *Answer choices:*

(see index for correct answer)

- a. International Symposium on Computer Architecture

- b. Harvard architecture
- c. Memory disambiguation
- d. abstraction level

Guidance: level 1

:: System administration ::

A _____ is a system monitor program used to provide information about the processes and applications running on a computer, as well as the general status of the computer. Some implementations can also be used to terminate processes and applications, as well as change the processes' scheduling priority. In some environments, users can access a _____ with the Control-Alt-Delete keyboard shortcut.

Exam Probability: **High**

46. *Answer choices:*

(see index for correct answer)

- a. OneSIS
- b. IBM LUM
- c. Task manager
- d. Sysload Software

Guidance: level 1

:: Computer architecture ::

In computer architecture, _____ is a technique that abstracts logical registers from physical registers. Every logical register has a set of physical registers associated with it. While a programmer in assembly language refers for instance to a logical register <code>accu</code>, the processor transposes this name to one specific physical register on the fly. The physical registers are opaque and can not be referenced directly but only via the canonical names.

Exam Probability: **Medium**

47. *Answer choices:*
(see index for correct answer)

- a. Memory ordering
- b. Abstraction layer
- c. Xorro
- d. Register renaming

Guidance: level 1

:: Computer architecture ::

A _____ processor is a CPU that implements a form of parallelism called instruction-level parallelism within a single processor. In contrast to a scalar processor that can execute at most one single instruction per clock cycle, a _____ processor can execute more than one instruction during a clock cycle by simultaneously dispatching multiple instructions to different execution units on the processor. It therefore allows for more throughput than would otherwise be possible at a given clock rate. Each execution unit is not a separate processor , but an execution resource within a single CPU such as an arithmetic logic unit.

Exam Probability: **High**

48. *Answer choices:*

(see index for correct answer)

- a. Instruction window
- b. Harvard architecture
- c. Superscalar
- d. Dataflow architecture

Guidance: level 1

:: Distributed computing architecture ::

In computer science, _____ is memory that may be simultaneously accessed by multiple programs with an intent to provide communication among them or avoid redundant copies. _____ is an efficient means of passing data between programs. Depending on context, programs may run on a single processor or on multiple separate processors.

Exam Probability: **High**

49. *Answer choices:*

(see index for correct answer)

- a. Shared memory
- b. Distributed lock manager
- c. Tuple space
- d. Distributed shared memory

Guidance: level 1

:: Computer file formats ::

The _____ format is an informal standard for configuration files for some computing platforms or software. _____ s are simple text files with a basic structure composed of sections, properties, and values.

Exam Probability: **Low**

50. *Answer choices:*

(see index for correct answer)

- a. Rich Text Format Directory
- b. INI file
- c. System Deployment Image
- d. Extended Log Format

Guidance: level 1

:: Central processing unit ::

A _____ is a processor register which changes or controls the general behavior of a CPU or other digital device. Common tasks performed by _____ s include interrupt control, switching the addressing mode, paging control, and coprocessor control.

Exam Probability: **Medium**

51. *Answer choices:*

(see index for correct answer)

- a. Control register
- b. Wait state
- c. Computer cooling
- d. Accumulator

Guidance: level 1

:: Computer storage buses ::

_____ is a feature of computer systems that allows certain hardware subsystems to access main system memory, independent of the central processing unit.

Exam Probability: **Medium**

52. *Answer choices:*

(see index for correct answer)

- a. Storage Module Device
- b. Direct memory access
- c. USB mass storage device class
- d. ST-506

Guidance: level 1

:: Digital typography ::

International Business Machines Corporation is an American multinational information technology company headquartered in Armonk, New York, with operations in over 170 countries. The company began in 1911, founded in Endicott, New York, as the Computing-Tabulating-Recording Company and was renamed "International Business Machines" in 1924.

Exam Probability: **High**

53. *Answer choices:*

(see index for correct answer)

- a. IBM
- b. Font substitution
- c. Vector font
- d. TeX font metric

Guidance: level 1

:: Servers (computing) ::

In computing, a _____ is a computer attached to a network that provides a location for shared disk access, i.e. shared storage of computer files that can be accessed by the workstations that are able to reach the computer that shares the access through a computer network. The term server highlights the role of the machine in the client–server scheme, where the clients are the workstations using the storage. It is common that a _____ does not perform computational tasks, and does not run programs on behalf of its clients.It is designed primarily to enable the storage and retrieval of data while the computation is carried out by the workstations.

Exam Probability: **High**

54. *Answer choices:*

(see index for correct answer)

- a. Windows Home Server
- b. File server
- c. BDII

- d. X Font Server

Guidance: level 1

:: Physical layer protocols ::

In telecommunications and computer networks, _____ is a method by which multiple analog or digital signals are combined into one signal over a shared medium. The aim is to share a scarce resource. For example, in telecommunications, several telephone calls may be carried using one wire. _____ originated in telegraphy in the 1870s, and is now widely applied in communications. In telephony, George Owen Squier is credited with the development of telephone carrier _____ in 1910.

Exam Probability: **High**

55. *Answer choices:*

(see index for correct answer)

- a. Multiplexing
- b. LocalTalk-to-Ethernet bridge
- c. IEEE 802.3
- d. RS-449

Guidance: level 1

:: Philosophical logic ::

_____ is the pattern of narrative development that aims to make vivid a place, object, character, or group. _____ is one of four rhetorical modes, along with exposition, argumentation, and narration. In practice it would be difficult to write literature that drew on just one of the four basic modes.

Exam Probability: **High**

56. *Answer choices:*

(see index for correct answer)

- a. Description
- b. Association for Logic, Language and Information
- c. Slingshot argument
- d. Deontic logic

Guidance: level 1

:: Formal languages ::

A _____ is a mark, sign or word that indicates, signifies, or is understood as representing an idea, object, or relationship. _____ s allow people to go beyond what is known or seen by creating linkages between otherwise very different concepts and experiences. All communication is achieved through the use of _____ s. _____ s take the form of words, sounds, gestures, ideas or visual images and are used to convey other ideas and beliefs. For example, a red octagon may be a _____ for "STOP". On a map, a blue line might represent a river. Numerals are _____ s for numbers. Alphabetic letters may be _____ s for sounds. Personal names are _____ s representing individuals. A red rose may _____ ize love and compassion. The variable 'x', in a mathematical equation, may _____ ize the position of a particle in space.

Exam Probability: **High**

57. *Answer choices:*

(see index for correct answer)

- a. Deterministic context-free language
- b. Symbol
- c. Regular grammar
- d. Bigram

Guidance: level 1

:: Central processing unit ::

In computer engineering, _____ is a set of rules and methods that describe the functionality, organization, and implementation of computer systems. Some definitions of architecture define it as describing the capabilities and programming model of a computer but not a particular implementation. In other definitions _____ involves instruction set architecture design, microarchitecture design, logic design, and implementation.

Exam Probability: **Low**

58. *Answer choices:*

(see index for correct answer)

- a. Tile processor
- b. Link register
- c. CPU locking
- d. Byte addressing

Guidance: level 1

:: Local area networks ::

_____ local area network technology is a communications protocol for local area networks. It uses a special three-byte frame called a "token" that travels around a logical "ring" of workstations or servers. This token passing is a channel access method providing fair access for all stations, and eliminating the collisions of contention-based access methods.

Exam Probability: **Medium**

59. *Answer choices:*

(see index for correct answer)

- a. Serial over LAN
- b. Ocarina Networks
- c. Token ring
- d. Fiber Distributed Data Interface

Guidance: level 1

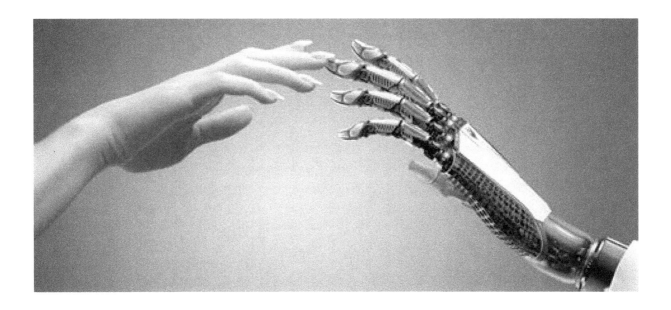

Human-computer interaction

Human–computer interaction researches the design and use of computer technology, focused on the interfaces between people (users) and computers. Researchers in the field of HCI both observe the ways in which humans interact with computers and design technologies that let humans interact with computers in novel ways. As a field of research, human–computer interaction is situated at the intersection of computer science, behavioral sciences, design, media studies, and several other fields of study.

:: User interfaces ::

A fat client is a computer, in client–server architecture or networks, that typically provides rich functionality independent of the central server. Originally known as just a "client" or "thick client," the name is contrasted to thin client, which describes a computer heavily dependent on a server's applications. A fat client may be described as having a _____ .

Exam Probability: **Low**

1. *Answer choices:*

(see index for correct answer)

- a. Web Dynpro
- b. Command history
- c. Aaron Marcus
- d. User experience

Guidance: level 1

:: Human–computer interaction ::

_____ is a user-centered design research method, part of the contextual design methodology. A _____ interview is usually structured as an approximately two-hour, one-on-one interaction in which the researcher watches the user in the course of the user's normal activities and discusses those activities with the user.

Exam Probability: **Low**

2. *Answer choices:*

(see index for correct answer)

- a. Turnaround document
- b. Contextual inquiry

- c. Interactive machine translation
- d. 3Dconnexion

Guidance: level 1

:: Raster graphics editors ::

_____ is any pigmented liquid, liquefiable, or mastic composition that, after application to a substrate in a thin layer, converts to a solid film. It is most commonly used to protect, color, or provide texture to objects. _____ can be made or purchased in many colors—and in many different types, such as watercolor, synthetic, etc. _____ is typically stored, sold, and applied as a liquid, but most types dry into a solid.

Exam Probability: **High**

3. *Answer choices:*

(see index for correct answer)

- a. GraphicConverter
- b. LView
- c. NEOchrome
- d. Photogenics

Guidance: level 1

:: User interfaces ::

A _____ is a graphical control element which poses an information area typically found at the window's bottom. It can be divided into sections to group information. Its job is primarily to display information about the current state of its window, although some _____ s have extra functionality. For example, many web browsers have clickable sections that pop up a display of security or privacy information.

Exam Probability: **High**

4. *Answer choices:*

(see index for correct answer)

- a. Natural language user interface
- b. Flight envelope protection
- c. MachPanel
- d. Object-oriented user interface

Guidance: level 1

:: Virtual reality ::

_____ is a technique in computer graphics for simulating bumps and wrinkles on the surface of an object. This is achieved by perturbing the surface normals of the object and using the perturbed normal during lighting calculations. The result is an apparently bumpy surface rather than a smooth surface although the surface of the underlying object is not changed. _____ was introduced by James Blinn in 1978.

Exam Probability: **High**

5. *Answer choices:*

(see index for correct answer)

- a. Sculpted prim
- b. DirectX
- c. SIMNET
- d. Bump mapping

Guidance: level 1

:: Ubiquitous computing ::

Ken Sakamura, as of April 2017 is a Japanese professor and dean of the Faculty of Information Networking for Innovation and Design at Toyo University, Japan. He is a former professor in Information science at the University of Tokyo. He is the creator of the real-time operating system architecture TRON.

Exam Probability: **Medium**

6. *Answer choices:*

(see index for correct answer)

- a. Ubiquitous commerce
- b. Ubiquitous Communicator
- c. Electronic leash

- d. SUBE card

Guidance: level 1

:: Computing input devices ::

In computing, an _____ is a piece of computer hardware equipment used to provide data and control signals to an information processing system such as a computer or information appliance. Examples of _____ s include keyboards, mouse, scanners, digital cameras and joysticks. Audio _____ s may be used for purposes including speech recognition. Many companies are utilizing speech recognition to help assist users to use their device.

Exam Probability: **Low**

7. *Answer choices:*

(see index for correct answer)

- a. Manual pulse generator
- b. TWAIN
- c. Apple Mouse
- d. CueCat

Guidance: level 1

:: Content management systems ::

_____ is the textual, visual, or aural content that is encountered as part of the user experience on websites. It may include—among other things—text, images, sounds, videos, and animations.

Exam Probability: **High**

8. *Answer choices:*

(see index for correct answer)

- a. Web content
- b. Papyrus Platform
- c. Elcom Technology
- d. EXo Platform

Guidance: level 1

:: User interface techniques ::

A voice-user interface makes spoken human interaction with computers possible, using speech recognition to understand spoken commands and questions, and typically text to speech to play a reply. A voice command device is a device controlled with a _____ .

Exam Probability: **Medium**

9. *Answer choices:*

(see index for correct answer)

- a. Mouse warping
- b. Gamification
- c. SmartAction
- d. Scroll wheel

Guidance: level 1

:: Computing input devices ::

_____ and _____ Direct are application programming interfaces and communication protocols that regulate communication between software and digital imaging devices, such as image scanners and digital cameras.

Exam Probability: **High**

10. *Answer choices:*

(see index for correct answer)

- a. Digital pen
- b. TREVENTUS
- c. Miburi
- d. TWAIN

Guidance: level 1

:: World Wide Web ::

A pageview or _____ , abbreviated in business to PV and occasionally called page impression, is a request to load a single HTML file of an Internet site. On the World Wide Web, a page request would result from a web surfer clicking on a link on another "page" pointing to the page in question.

Exam Probability: **High**

11. *Answer choices:*

(see index for correct answer)

- a. Webcare
- b. Traffic exchange
- c. Rockto
- d. Page view

Guidance: level 1

:: User interfaces ::

The _____, in the industrial design field of human–computer interaction, is the space where interactions between humans and machines occur. The goal of this interaction is to allow effective operation and control of the machine from the human end, whilst the machine simultaneously feeds back information that aids the operators' decision-making process. Examples of this broad concept of _____ s include the interactive aspects of computer operating systems, hand tools, heavy machinery operator controls, and process controls. The design considerations applicable when creating _____ s are related to or involve such disciplines as ergonomics and psychology.

Exam Probability: **Low**

12. *Answer choices:*

(see index for correct answer)

- a. Rich user interaction
- b. User interface
- c. Object-oriented user interface
- d. Desktop metaphor

Guidance: level 1

:: Human–computer interaction ::

_____ is a brand name associated with the development of the _____ web browser. It is now owned by Verizon Media, a subsidiary of Verizon. The brand belonged to the _____ Communications Corporation, an independent American computer services company, whose headquarters were in Mountain View, California, and later Dulles, Virginia. The browser was once dominant but lost to Internet Explorer and other competitors after the so-called first browser war, its market share falling from more than 90 percent in the mid-1990s to less than 1 percent in 2006.

Exam Probability: **Low**

13. *Answer choices:*

(see index for correct answer)

- a. Gulf of execution
- b. Ambiguous computing
- c. Reading path
- d. Interactive machine translation

Guidance: level 1

:: Computing input devices ::

A _____ is a computer that interacts with the user through the surface of an ordinary object, rather than through a monitor, keyboard, mouse, or other physical hardware.

Exam Probability: **Medium**

14. *Answer choices:*

(see index for correct answer)

- a. Frame grabber
- b. Optical trackpad
- c. Logitech G25
- d. Surface computer

Guidance: level 1

:: Ergonomics ::

_____ is an engineering discipline using computers to solve complex ergonomic problems involving interaction between the human body and its environment. The human body holds a great complexity thus it can be beneficial to use computers to solve problems involving the human body and the environment that surrounds it.

Exam Probability: **Medium**

15. *Answer choices:*

(see index for correct answer)

- a. Sports engineering
- b. Computer-aided ergonomics
- c. High-velocity human factors
- d. Lift table

Guidance: level 1

:: History of the Internet ::

SRI International's _____ was founded in the 1960s by electrical engineer Douglas Engelbart to develop and experiment with new tools and techniques for collaboration and information processing.

Exam Probability: **Medium**

16. *Answer choices:*

(see index for correct answer)

- a. North American Network Operators%27 Group
- b. Wayback Machine
- c. Augmentation Research Center
- d. AMSD Ariadna

Guidance: level 1

:: Ergonomics ::

_____ is the design of products, devices, services, or environments for people with disabilities. The concept of accessible design and practice of accessible development ensures both "direct access" and "indirect access" meaning compatibility with a person's assistive technology.

Exam Probability: **High**

17. *Answer choices:*

(see index for correct answer)

- a. Needs analysis
- b. Accessibility
- c. Kneeling chair
- d. Lift table

Guidance: level 1

:: World Wide Web ::

_____ is the continuing process used by webmasters to improve content and increase exposure of a website to bring more visitors. Many techniques such as search engine optimization and search engine submission are used to increase a site's traffic once content is developed.

Exam Probability: **Low**

18. *Answer choices:*

(see index for correct answer)

- a. Website governance
- b. Website promotion
- c. Digital Sky Technologies
- d. Backlink

Guidance: level 1

:: World Wide Web ::

An online _____ is a "Yellow Pages-Style" web directory that specializes in ecommerce sites. Inspired by the organizational structure used in traditional shopping mall directories, online shopping directories organize ecommerce sites by their category and subcategory of goods sold. Without the constraints related to shopping at a physical mall, an online _____ serves to aggregate all ecommerce sites in one centralized location in order to help a user decide where to shop online.

Exam Probability: **High**

19. *Answer choices:*

(see index for correct answer)

- a. Framekiller
- b. Deep Web
- c. Webometrics
- d. Shopping directory

Guidance: level 1

:: Photo software ::

_____ is a raster graphics editor developed and published by Adobe Inc. for Windows and macOS. It was originally created in 1988 by Thomas and John Knoll. Since then, this software has become the industry standard not only in raster graphics editing, but in digital art as a whole. The software's name has thus become a generic trademark, leading to its usage as a verb although Adobe discourages such use. Photoshop can edit and compose raster images in multiple layers and supports masks, alpha compositing, and several color models including RGB, CMYK, CIELAB, spot color, and duotone. Photoshop uses its own <code>PSD</code> and <code>PSB</code> file formats to support these features. In addition to raster graphics, this software has limited abilities to edit or render text and vector graphics, as well as 3D graphics and video. Its feature set can be expanded by plug-ins; programs developed and distributed independently of Photoshop that run inside it and offer new or enhanced features.

Exam Probability: **Low**

20. *Answer choices:*
(see index for correct answer)

- a. Adobe Photoshop
- b. Noise Ninja
- c. Picture Motion Browser
- d. PhotoPerfect

Guidance: level 1

:: User interfaces ::

A _____ is a usability inspection method for computer software that helps to identify usability problems in the user interface design. It specifically involves evaluators examining the interface and judging its compliance with recognized usability principles . These evaluation methods are now widely taught and practiced in the new media sector, where UIs are often designed in a short space of time on a budget that may restrict the amount of money available to provide for other types of interface testing.

Exam Probability: **Low**

21. *Answer choices:*

(see index for correct answer)

- a. Aaron Marcus
- b. Sparsh
- c. Heuristic evaluation
- d. Exocentric environment

Guidance: level 1

:: Automatic identification and data capture ::

_____ is the trademark for a type of matrix barcode first designed in 1994 for the automotive industry in Japan. A barcode is a machine-readable optical label that contains information about the item to which it is attached. In practice, _____ s often contain data for a locator, identifier, or tracker that points to a website or application. A _____ uses four standardized encoding modes to store data efficiently; extensions may also be used.

Exam Probability: **Low**

22. *Answer choices:*

(see index for correct answer)

- a. Bokode
- b. Magnadata Group
- c. QR Code
- d. CyberCode

Guidance: level 1

:: Computing input devices ::

Smart Technologies Corporation is a Canadian company headquartered in Calgary, Alberta, Canada. Founded in 1987, Smart Technologies is best known as the developer of interactive whiteboards branded as " _____ s".

Exam Probability: **Low**

23. *Answer choices:*

(see index for correct answer)

- a. SMART Board
- b. Digital pen
- c. Controller-free motion control
- d. CrossPad

Guidance: level 1

:: Virtual reality ::

The user interface, in the industrial design field of human–computer interaction, is the space where interactions between humans and machines occur. The goal of this interaction is to allow effective operation and control of the machine from the human end, whilst the machine simultaneously feeds back information that aids the operators' decision-making process. Examples of this broad concept of user interfaces include the interactive aspects of computer operating systems, hand tools, heavy machinery operator controls, and process controls. The design considerations applicable when creating user interfaces are related to or involve such disciplines as ergonomics and psychology.

Exam Probability: **Medium**

24. *Answer choices:*

(see index for correct answer)

- a. Mark Stephen Meadows
- b. Lifelike experience

- c. Virtual user interface
- d. Tony Parisi

Guidance: level 1

:: Ergonomics ::

_____ or balanced sitting includes a sitting posture that approaches the natural resting position. A forward sloping seat encourages this natural posture, which is the same as when lying on the side while sleeping. The lumbar curve is preserved, the joint angles are open, and muscles are well-balanced and relaxed. This position is exactly the same as when riding a horse: the rider sits upright and at the same time maintains a lumbar lordosis because of the downwards sloping thighs.

Exam Probability: **High**

25. *Answer choices:*
(see index for correct answer)

- a. CEN/CENELEC Guide 6
- b. Riding-like sitting
- c. Neuroergonomics
- d. Use-centered design

Guidance: level 1

:: User interfaces ::

_____ is the practice of presenting information in a way that fosters efficient and effective understanding of it. The term has come to be used specifically for graphic design for displaying information effectively, rather than just attractively or for artistic expression. _____ is closely related to the field of data visualization and is often taught as part of graphic design courses.

Exam Probability: **Low**

26. *Answer choices:*

(see index for correct answer)

- a. Virtual console
- b. Direct mode
- c. Information design
- d. Multi-monitor

Guidance: level 1

:: Usability ::

In computing, a _____ is a file manager that uses a spatial metaphor to represent files and folders as if they are real physical objects.

Exam Probability: **High**

27. *Answer choices:*

(see index for correct answer)

- a. Usage-centered design
- b. Questionnaire for User Interaction Satisfaction
- c. Usability testing
- d. Jaime Levy

Guidance: level 1

:: Virtual reality ::

_____ is a virtual reality device. It is, as the name suggests, spherical. It consists of a 10-foot hollow sphere, which is placed on a special platform that allows the sphere to rotate freely in any direction according to the user's steps. It works with computer based simulations and virtual worlds, and rotates as the user walks, allowing for an unlimited plane upon which the user can walk. A wireless head-mounted display with gyroscopes is used to both track the user's head movement as well as display the environment of the virtual world. _____ can serve many purposes, including exercise, video gaming, military training, and virtual museum tours.

Exam Probability: **Low**

28. *Answer choices:*

(see index for correct answer)

- a. 3D stereo view
- b. Virtual art

- c. Gran Turismo official steering wheel
- d. VirtuSphere

Guidance: level 1

:: Usability ::

_____ is a design methodology, which proposes a business centric approach for designing user interfaces. Because of the multi-stage business analysis steps involved right from the beginning of the PCD life cycle, it is believed to achieve the highest levels of business-IT alignment that is possible through UI.

Exam Probability: **High**

29. *Answer choices:*

(see index for correct answer)

- a. Process-centered design
- b. Look and feel
- c. Affinity diagram
- d. Eating your own dog food

Guidance: level 1

:: Computing input devices ::

_____ is a measurement of the resolution of an image scanner, in particular the number of individual samples that are taken in the space of one linear inch. It is sometimes misreferred to as dots per inch, though that term more accurately refers to printing resolution. Generally, the greater the SPI of a scanner, the more detailed its reproduction of the scanned object.

Exam Probability: **Medium**

30. *Answer choices:*

(see index for correct answer)

- a. Samples per inch
- b. Orbita mouse
- c. Optical mouse
- d. Capacitive sensing

Guidance: level 1

:: Mixed reality ::

_____ is the combining of visual elements from separate sources into single images, often to create the illusion that all those elements are parts of the same scene. Live-action shooting for _____ is variously called "chroma key", "blue screen", "green screen" and other names. Today, most, though not all, _____ is achieved through digital image manipulation. Pre-digital _____ techniques, however, go back as far as the trick films of Georges Méliès in the late 19th century, and some are still in use.

Exam Probability: **High**

31. *Answer choices:*

(see index for correct answer)

- a. Interactive video compositing
- b. Gbanga
- c. Bamzooki
- d. Compositing

Guidance: level 1

:: Speech recognition ::

_____ is the study of speech signals and the processing methods of signals. The signals are usually processed in a digital representation, so _____ can be regarded as a special case of digital signal processing, applied to speech signals. Aspects of _____ includes the acquisition, manipulation, storage, transfer and output of speech signals. The input is called speech recognition and the output is called speech synthesis.

Exam Probability: **Medium**

32. *Answer choices:*

(see index for correct answer)

- a. Speech processing
- b. Windows Speech Recognition

- c. IBM Shoebox
- d. Pattern playback

Guidance: level 1

:: Internet terminology ::

A _____ is a discussion or informational website published on the World Wide Web consisting of discrete, often informal diary-style text entries. Posts are typically displayed in reverse chronological order, so that the most recent post appears first, at the top of the web page. Until 2009, _____ s were usually the work of a single individual, occasionally of a small group, and often covered a single subject or topic. In the 2010s, "multi-author _____ s" emerged, featuring the writing of multiple authors and sometimes professionally edited. MABs from newspapers, other media outlets, universities, think tanks, advocacy groups, and similar institutions account for an increasing quantity of _____ traffic. The rise of Twitter and other "micro _____ ging" systems helps integrate MABs and single-author _____ s into the news media. _____ can also be used as a verb, meaning to maintain or add content to a _____ .

Exam Probability: **High**

33. *Answer choices:*

(see index for correct answer)

- a. Daily active users
- b. Premium Internet
- c. Social data analysis
- d. Blog

Guidance: level 1

:: Virtual reality ::

_____ is a technique used in remote reality to transfer the perception of one sense to another. For example, a thermographic camera allows us to have a visual sensation of the temperature, which is atypical thermoception.

Exam Probability: **Low**

34. *Answer choices:*
(see index for correct answer)

- a. Web3D Consortium
- b. TreadPort Active Wind Tunnel
- c. Sensorial transposition
- d. Perpetuum

Guidance: level 1

:: Usability ::

_____ is a technique used in user-centered interaction design to evaluate a product by testing it on users. This can be seen as an irreplaceable usability practice, since it gives direct input on how real users use the system. This is in contrast with usability inspection methods where experts use different methods to evaluate a user interface without involving users.

Exam Probability: **High**

35. *Answer choices:*

(see index for correct answer)

- a. Affinity diagram
- b. Usability testing
- c. User-centered design
- d. Look and feel

Guidance: level 1

:: Virtual reality ::

_____ is a technique used in 3D computer graphics to add lighting effects to a rendered scene. It allows the viewer to see beams of light shining through the environment; seeing sunbeams streaming through an open window is an example of _____, also known as crepuscular rays. The term seems to have been introduced from cinematography and is now widely applied to 3D modelling and rendering especially in the field of 3D gaming.

Exam Probability: **Low**

36. *Answer choices:*

(see index for correct answer)

- a. Volumetric lighting
- b. FORAN System
- c. BattleTech Centers
- d. Cyberwar

Guidance: level 1

:: World Wide Web ::

Separation of content and presentation is the separation of concerns design principle as applied to the authoring and presentation of content. Under this principle, visual and design aspects are separated from the core material and structure of a document. A typical analogy used to explain this principle is the distinction between the human skeleton and human flesh which makes up the body's appearance. Common applications of this principle are seen in Web design and markup language.

Exam Probability: **Medium**

37. *Answer choices:*

(see index for correct answer)

- a. Stanford Web Credibility Project
- b. Humans.txt
- c. Separation of presentation and content

- d. Guillaume Besse

Guidance: level 1

:: Virtual reality ::

In 3D computer graphics, _____, or Dot3 bump mapping, is a technique used for faking the lighting of bumps and dents – an implementation of bump mapping. It is used to add details without using more polygons. A common use of this technique is to greatly enhance the appearance and details of a low polygon model by generating a normal map from a high polygon model or height map.

Exam Probability: **High**

38. *Answer choices:*

(see index for correct answer)

- a. PhysX
- b. Simulation hypothesis
- c. Telepointer
- d. GT Racing Cockpit

Guidance: level 1

:: History of human–computer interaction ::

A voice-user interface makes spoken human interaction with computers possible, using speech recognition to understand spoken commands and questions, and typically text to speech to play a reply. A _____ is a device controlled with a voice user interface.

Exam Probability: **Low**

39. *Answer choices:*

(see index for correct answer)

- a. Microsoft PixelSense
- b. Sketchpad
- c. File Retrieval and Editing System
- d. Voice command device

Guidance: level 1

:: Software requirements ::

A _____ is a representation of a system, made of the composition of concepts which are used to help people know, understand, or simulate a subject the model represents. It is also a set of concepts. Some models are physical objects; for example, a toy model which may be assembled, and may be made to work like the object it represents.

Exam Probability: **High**

40. *Answer choices:*

(see index for correct answer)

- a. ERequirements
- b. Product requirements document
- c. Conceptual model
- d. Requirements analysis

Guidance: level 1

:: Natural language and computing ::

_____ or complex text rendering is the typesetting of writing systems in which the shape or positioning of a grapheme depends on its relation to other graphemes. The term is used in the field of software internationalization, where each grapheme is a character.

Exam Probability: **Medium**

41. *Answer choices:*

(see index for correct answer)

- a. Internet linguistics
- b. Complex text layout
- c. Input method
- d. Han unification

Guidance: level 1

:: Computer graphics ::

In computer displays, filmmaking, television production, and other kinetic displays, _____ is sliding text, images or video across a monitor or display, vertically or horizontally. "_____," as such, does not change the layout of the text or pictures but moves the user's view across what is apparently a larger image that is not wholly seen. A common television and movie special effect is to scroll credits, while leaving the background stationary. _____ may take place completely without user intervention or, on an interactive device, be triggered by touchscreen or a keypress and continue without further intervention until a further user action, or be entirely controlled by input devices.

Exam Probability: **High**

42. *Answer choices:*

(see index for correct answer)

- a. Visual artifact
- b. Cybernetic Serendipity
- c. NAPLPS
- d. Channel

Guidance: level 1

:: Virtual reality ::

Second Life is an online virtual world, developed and owned by the San Francisco-based firm Linden Lab and launched on June 23, 2003. By 2013, Second Life had approximately one million regular users; at the end of 2017 active user count totals "between 800,000 and 900,000". In many ways, Second Life is similar to massively multiplayer online role-playing games; however, Linden Lab is emphatic that their creation is not a game: "There is no manufactured conflict, no set objective".

Exam Probability: **High**

43. *Answer choices:*

(see index for correct answer)

- a. Immersive virtual musical instrument
- b. Cyberwar
- c. Perpetuum
- d. Stereotaxy

Guidance: level 1

:: User interfaces ::

_____ is a commercial web hosting platform with a control panel that allows a server administrator to set up new websites, reseller accounts, e-mail accounts and DNS entries through a web-based interface.

Exam Probability: **Medium**

44. Answer choices:

(see index for correct answer)

- a. Video wall
- b. Laster Technologies
- c. Reactable
- d. Plesk

Guidance: level 1

:: Internet terminology ::

A _____ is a thin marker, commonly made of card, leather, or fabric, used to keep the reader's place in a book and to enable the reader to return to it with ease. Other frequently used materials for _____ s are paper, metals like silver and brass, silk, wood, cord , and plastic. Many _____ s can be clipped on a page with the aid of a page-flap.

Exam Probability: **Medium**

45. Answer choices:

(see index for correct answer)

- a. Crowdfunding
- b. Search engine marketing
- c. Bookmark
- d. Web widget

Guidance: level 1

:: Computer network security ::

_____ is software that aims to gather information about a person or organization, sometimes without their knowledge, that may send such information to another entity without the consumer's consent, that asserts control over a device without the consumer's knowledge, or it may send such information to another entity with the consumer's consent, through cookies.

Exam Probability: **Low**

46. *Answer choices:*

(see index for correct answer)

- a. Attack tree
- b. AEGIS SecureConnect
- c. OCML
- d. Spyware

Guidance: level 1

:: Virtual reality ::

_____ was initially the idea to fully display and navigate Web sites using 3D. By extension, the term now refers to all interactive 3D content which are embedded into web pages' HTML, and that users can see through a web browser.

Exam Probability: **Medium**

47. *Answer choices:*

(see index for correct answer)

- a. Virtual environment software
- b. Endocentric environment
- c. Web3D
- d. Virtual Reality and Education Laboratory

Guidance: level 1

:: World Wide Web ::

_____, web harvesting, or web data extraction is data scraping used for extracting data from websites. _____ software may access the World Wide Web directly using the Hypertext Transfer Protocol, or through a web browser. While _____ can be done manually by a software user, the term typically refers to automated processes implemented using a bot or web crawler. It is a form of copying, in which specific data is gathered and copied from the web, typically into a central local database or spreadsheet, for later retrieval or analysis.

Exam Probability: **Low**

48. *Answer choices:*

(see index for correct answer)

- a. Web scraping
- b. Traffic exchange
- c. Rule Interchange Format
- d. Linked data

Guidance: level 1

:: Virtual reality ::

_____ is an experience taking place within simulated and immersive environments that can be similar to or completely different from the real world. Applications of _____ can include entertainment and educational purposes. Other, distinct types of VR style technology include augmented reality and mixed reality.

Exam Probability: **Medium**

49. *Answer choices:*

(see index for correct answer)

- a. Open Inventor
- b. Volumetric lighting

- c. Virtual reality therapy
- d. Maurice Benayoun

Guidance: level 1

:: Graphical user interface elements ::

In computer interface design, a _____ is a graphical control element on which on-screen buttons, icons, menus, or other input or output elements are placed. _____ s are seen in many types of software such as office suites, graphics editors and web browsers. _____ s are usually distinguished from palettes by their integration into the edges of the screen or larger windows, which results in wasted space if too many underpopulated bars are stacked atop each other or interface inefficiency if overloaded bars are placed on small windows.

Exam Probability: **Medium**

50. *Answer choices:*

(see index for correct answer)

- a. Pop-up notification
- b. Balloon help
- c. Toolbar
- d. Adjustment handles

Guidance: level 1

:: Software design ::

Design can refer to such a plan or specification or to the created object, etc., and features of it such as aesthetic, functional, economic or socio-political.

Exam Probability: **Low**

51. *Answer choices:*
(see index for correct answer)

- a. Blinking twelve problem
- b. functional model
- c. Design rationale
- d. Oslo

Guidance: level 1

:: Graphical user interfaces ::

A multiple document interface is a graphical user interface in which multiple windows reside under a single parent window. Such systems often allow child windows to embed other windows inside them as well, creating complex nested hierarchies. This contrasts with _____ s where all windows are independent of each other.

Exam Probability: **Medium**

52. *Answer choices:*

(see index for correct answer)

- a. StyleXP
- b. CEGUI
- c. Adaptive user interface
- d. Single document interface

Guidance: level 1

:: Virtual reality ::

_____ is a computer-enhanced methodology used to assess behavioral and physiological reactivity to drug and alcohol sensory cues. Studies indicate that cue reactivity—a response to the presentation of various visual, auditory, olfactory, and tactile cues—increases physiological excitement in addicts. VRCR utilizes virtual reality technology to stimulate cue reactivity in the most efficient and realistic environments possible; the intention being that coping skills can be taught in a contextual scenario that reflect a real world situation. While still in the early stages of development, studies have shown that VRCR is an effective means of generating a craving-inspiring environment that is tempting to a patient suffering from addiction.

Exam Probability: **Medium**

53. *Answer choices:*

(see index for correct answer)

- a. Virtual reality cue reactivity

- b. Cave5D
- c. Battlezone
- d. Virtual heritage

Guidance: level 1

:: Healthcare software ::

The Veterans Information Systems and Technology Architecture is the nationwide veterans clinical and business information system of the U.S. Department of Veterans Affairs. _____ consists of 180 applications for clinical, financial, and administrative functions all integrated within a single database, providing single, authoritative source of data for all veteran-related care and services. The U.S. Congress mandates the VA keep the veterans health record in a single, authoritative, lifelong database, which is _____ .

Exam Probability: **High**

54. *Answer choices:*
(see index for correct answer)

- a. Composite Health Care System
- b. Patient administration system
- c. Electronic Distributed Monitoring and Evaluation Solution
- d. VistA

Guidance: level 1

:: Virtual reality ::

_____ are girl dolls manufactured by Ty Inc. Similar to the Ty Beanie Babies the _____ are on a limited release pattern with dolls being introduced and older ones retired at various times. _____ are plush toys that are connected to an online virtual world at TyGirlz.com. Introduced to the global market on April 13, 2007, _____ was one of only a few virtual worlds geared to girls. The line was discontinued in 2013 and the virtual world shut down on June 7 of that same year.

Exam Probability: **Low**

55. *Answer choices:*
(see index for correct answer)

- a. Id Tech 5
- b. Ty Girlz
- c. Amateur flight simulation
- d. Virtual reality

Guidance: level 1

:: Speech recognition ::

_____ Rapid Open Source Intelligence Deployment System, which timeshifts the video then processes speech-to-text through the SAIL LABS Technology automatic speech recognition and then hands the XML result to a machine translation engine. The translated text is then resynchronized with the video and the result is translated close caption in real time. The idea originated after a request of a Navy to deploy these systems on board ships in order to be aware of what is being said on television stations close to the ship's route or at the port of call. It was later used in peace keeping solutions. In 2007 the inventing team from SAIL LABS Technology won the European ICT Prize.

Exam Probability: **Low**

56. *Answer choices:*

(see index for correct answer)

- a. Natural language processing
- b. ROSIDS
- c. Telesoft Technologies
- d. Silent speech interface

Guidance: level 1

:: Image processing ::

_____ is an ability of animals to perceive differences between light composed of different wavelengths independently of light intensity. The perception is a part of the larger vision system and is mediated by a complex process between neurons that begins with differential stimulation of different types of photoreceptors by light entering the eye. Those photoreceptors then emit outputs that are then propagated through many layers of neurons and then ultimately to the brain. _____ is found in many animals and is mediated by similar underlying mechanisms with common types of biological molecules and a complex history of evolution in different animal taxa. In primates, _____ may have evolved to under selective pressure for a variety of visual tasks including the foraging for nutritious young leaves, ripe fruit and flowers as well as detecting predator camouflage and emotional states in other primates.

Exam Probability: **Low**

57. *Answer choices:*

(see index for correct answer)

- a. Edge enhancement
- b. Adaptive histogram equalization
- c. Signal transfer function
- d. Boundary vector field

Guidance: level 1

:: Debuggers ::

_____ is the process of finding and resolving defects or problems within a computer program that prevent correct operation of computer software or a system.

Exam Probability: **Low**

58. *Answer choices:*

(see index for correct answer)

- a. Debugging
- b. Debugger
- c. WinDbg
- d. Dprobes

Guidance: level 1

:: Automatic identification and data capture ::

A _____ is an implementation of the MIFARE RFID chip, encased in a plastic key style housing. It is used as a prepayment system on vending machines and for some self-service diving air compressors in Switzerland

Exam Probability: **Medium**

59. *Answer choices:*

(see index for correct answer)

- a. Burst transmission
- b. Omni-ID
- c. U-Key
- d. Intermec

Guidance: level 1

Software engineering

Software engineering include is the systematic application of scientific and technological knowledge, methods, and experience to the design, implementation, testing, and documentation of software

---

:: Programming language implementation ::

An _____, often abbreviated asm, is any low-level programming language in which there is a very strong correspondence between the program's statements and the architecture's machine code instructions.

Exam Probability: **Low**

1. *Answer choices:*

(see index for correct answer)

- a. Assembly language
- b. Aspect weaver
- c. Exe2bin
- d. Lexical analysis

Guidance: level 1

:: Control flow ::

In computer science, _____ is the order in which individual statements, instructions or function calls of an imperative program are executed or evaluated. The emphasis on explicit _____ distinguishes an imperative programming language from a declarative programming language.

Exam Probability: **Low**

2. *Answer choices:*

(see index for correct answer)

- a. Continuation
- b. while loop

Guidance: level 1

:: Programming language topics ::

A _____ is a formal language, which comprises a set of instructions that produce various kinds of output. _____ s are used in computer programming to implement algorithms.

Exam Probability: **High**

3. *Answer choices:*

(see index for correct answer)

- a. Programming language
- b. Exception safety
- c. Software transactional memory
- d. Leaning toothpick syndrome

Guidance: level 1

:: Raster graphics editors ::

_____ is any pigmented liquid, liquefiable, or mastic composition that, after application to a substrate in a thin layer, converts to a solid film. It is most commonly used to protect, color, or provide texture to objects. _____ can be made or purchased in many colors—and in many different types, such as watercolor, synthetic, etc. _____ is typically stored, sold, and applied as a liquid, but most types dry into a solid.

Exam Probability: **High**

4. *Answer choices:*

(see index for correct answer)

- a. LView
- b. Paint
- c. Brilliance
- d. Adobe Photoshop Elements

Guidance: level 1

:: Graphics file formats ::

_____ is a commonly used method of lossy compression for digital images, particularly for those images produced by digital photography. The degree of compression can be adjusted, allowing a selectable tradeoff between storage size and image quality. _____ typically achieves 10:1 compression with little perceptible loss in image quality.

Exam Probability: **Low**

5. *Answer choices:*

(see index for correct answer)

- a. Graphics Interchange Format
- b. Alembic
- c. JPEG
- d. Vector graphics

Guidance: level 1

:: Software engineering ::

_____ is the capability to trace something. In some cases, it is interpreted as the ability to verify the history, location, or application of an item by means of documented recorded identification.

Exam Probability: **Low**

6. *Answer choices:*

(see index for correct answer)

- a. Round-trip engineering
- b. Code reuse
- c. Value-based software engineering
- d. Traceability

Guidance: level 1

:: Computer graphics ::

_____ are visual images or designs on some surface, such as a wall, canvas, screen, paper, or stone to inform, illustrate, or entertain. In contemporary usage, it includes a pictorial representation of data, as in computer-aided design and manufacture, in typesetting and the graphic arts, and in educational and recreational software. Images that are generated by a computer are called computer _____ .

Exam Probability: **Low**

7. *Answer choices:*

(see index for correct answer)

- a. Retained mode
- b. Video overlay
- c. Visualization
- d. Blanking

Guidance: level 1

:: Systems analysis ::

A _____ in software engineering and organizational theory is a chart which shows the breakdown of a system to its lowest manageable levels. They are used in structured programming to arrange program modules into a tree. Each module is represented by a box, which contains the module's name. The tree structure visualizes the relationships between modules.

Exam Probability: **Medium**

8. *Answer choices:*

(see index for correct answer)

- a. HIPO
- b. Policy analysis
- c. Structure chart
- d. Earth system science

Guidance: level 1

:: Trees (data structures) ::

In computer science, _____ is a form of graph traversal and refers to the process of visiting each node in a tree data structure, exactly once. Such traversals are classified by the order in which the nodes are visited. The following algorithms are described for a binary tree, but they may be generalized to other trees as well.

Exam Probability: **High**

9. Answer choices:

(see index for correct answer)

- a. Split
- b. Leftist tree
- c. SPQR tree
- d. Tree traversal

Guidance: level 1

:: Programming libraries ::

A _____ in computer programming is the library made available across implementations of a programming language. These libraries are conventionally described in programming language specifications; however, contents of a language's associated library may also be determined by more informal practices of a language's community.

Exam Probability: **High**

10. Answer choices:

(see index for correct answer)

- a. OpenSC
- b. User Direct Access Programming Library

Guidance: level 1

:: Variable (computer programming) ::

In computer science, a _____ is a variable that is given local scope. _____ references in the function or block in which it is declared override the same variable name in the larger scope. In programming languages with only two levels of visibility, _____ s are contrasted with global variables. On the other hand, many ALGOL-derived languages allow any number of nested levels of visibility, with private variables, functions, constants and types hidden within them, either by nested blocks or nested functions. _____ s are fundamental to procedural programming, and more generally modular programming: variables of local scope are used to avoid issues with side-effects that can occur with global variables.

Exam Probability: **Medium**

11. *Answer choices:*
(see index for correct answer)

- a. class variable
- b. Global scope
- c. global variables
- d. Local variable

Guidance: level 1

:: Software engineering ::

A _____ is a system on intercommunicating components based on software forming part of a computer system. It "consists of a number of separate programs, configuration files, which are used to set up these programs, system documentation, which describes the structure of the system, and user documentation, which explains how to use the system".

Exam Probability: **High**

12. *Answer choices:*

(see index for correct answer)

- a. Software system
- b. Experimental software engineering
- c. Software development process
- d. Task-oriented information modelling

Guidance: level 1

:: Data management ::

_____ is "data [information] that provides information about other data". Many distinct types of _____ exist, among these descriptive _____, structural _____, administrative _____, reference _____ and statistical _____.

Exam Probability: **High**

13. *Answer choices:*

(see index for correct answer)

- a. Approximate inference
- b. DAMA
- c. World Wide Molecular Matrix
- d. Metadata

Guidance: level 1

:: Unified Modeling Language diagrams ::

A _____ shows object interactions arranged in time sequence. It depicts the objects and classes involved in the scenario and the sequence of messages exchanged between the objects needed to carry out the functionality of the scenario. _____ s are typically associated with use case realizations in the Logical View of the system under development. _____ s are sometimes called event diagrams or event scenarios.

Exam Probability: **High**

14. *Answer choices:*

(see index for correct answer)

- a. Object diagram
- b. Sequence diagram
- c. System sequence diagram
- d. Communication diagram

Guidance: level 1

:: Formal languages ::

In formal language theory and computer programming, string _____ is the operation of joining character strings end-to-end. For example, the _____ of "snow" and "ball" is "snowball". In some but not all formalisations of _____ theory, also called string theory, string _____ is a primitive notion.

Exam Probability: **Low**

15. *Answer choices:*

(see index for correct answer)

- a. Weighted context-free grammar
- b. Concatenation
- c. Cross-serial dependency
- d. Uniquely inversible grammar

Guidance: level 1

:: Data types ::

A _____, also called a subroutine pointer or procedure pointer, is a pointer that points to a function. As opposed to referencing a data value, a _____ points to executable code within memory. Dereferencing the _____ yields the referenced function, which can be invoked and passed arguments just as in a normal function call. Such an invocation is also known as an "indirect" call, because the function is being invoked indirectly through a variable instead of directly through a fixed identifier or address.

Exam Probability: **Low**

16. *Answer choices:*

(see index for correct answer)

- a. Top type
- b. Function pointer
- c. Cons
- d. Typing environment

Guidance: level 1

:: Naming conventions ::

In computing, a _____ is a set of symbols that are used to organize objects of various kinds, so that these objects may be referred to by name. In Java, a _____ ensures that all the identifiers within it must have unique names so that they can be easily identified. In order to manage the _____ Java provides the mechanism of creating Java packages. Prominent examples include.

Exam Probability: **Low**

17. *Answer choices:*

(see index for correct answer)

- a. Leszynski naming convention
- b. Namespace

Guidance: level 1

:: Control characters ::

_____ is the boundless three-dimensional extent in which objects and events have relative position and direction. Physical _____ is often conceived in three linear dimensions, although modern physicists usually consider it, with time, to be part of a boundless four-dimensional continuum known as _____ time. The concept of _____ is considered to be of fundamental importance to an understanding of the physical universe. However, disagreement continues between philosophers over whether it is itself an entity, a relationship between entities, or part of a conceptual framework.

Exam Probability: **Medium**

18. *Answer choices:*

(see index for correct answer)

- a. Block check character
- b. Space

- c. Zero-width non-joiner
- d. Line starve

Guidance: level 1

:: Computer data ::

A _____ is a kind of computer file that is structured as a sequence of lines of electronic text. A _____ exists stored as data within a computer file system. In operating systems such as CP/M and MS-DOS, where the operating system does not keep track of the file size in bytes, the end of a _____ is denoted by placing one or more special characters, known as an end-of-file marker, as padding after the last line in a _____. On modern operating systems such as Microsoft Windows and Unix-like systems, _____ s do not contain any special EOF character, because file systems on those operating systems keep track of the file size in bytes. There are for most _____ s a need to have end-of-line delimiters, which are done in a few different ways depending on operating system. Some operating systems with record-orientated file systems may not use new line delimiters and will primarily store _____ s with lines separated as fixed or variable length records.

Exam Probability: **High**

19. *Answer choices:*
(see index for correct answer)

- a. Text file
- b. Trailer
- c. Random access
- d. Data consistency

Guidance: level 1

:: Software development philosophies ::

_____ is a software development methodology which is intended to improve software quality and responsiveness to changing customer requirements. As a type of agile software development, it advocates frequent "releases" in short development cycles, which is intended to improve productivity and introduce checkpoints at which new customer requirements can be adopted.

Exam Probability: **Medium**

20. *Answer choices:*

(see index for correct answer)

- a. The Magic Cauldron
- b. Lean software development
- c. Unix philosophy
- d. Waterfall model

Guidance: level 1

:: Distributed computing architecture ::

In computer science, _____ is a technique for invoking behavior on a computer. The invoking program sends a message to a process and relies on the process and the supporting infrastructure to select and invoke the actual code to run. _____ differs from conventional programming where a process, subroutine, or function is directly invoked by name. _____ is key to some models of concurrency and object-oriented programming.

Exam Probability: **Medium**

21. *Answer choices:*

(see index for correct answer)

- a. Message passing
- b. Shared memory
- c. Distributed shared memory
- d. Tuple space

Guidance: level 1

:: Philosophical logic ::

_____ is the pattern of narrative development that aims to make vivid a place, object, character, or group. _____ is one of four rhetorical modes, along with exposition, argumentation, and narration. In practice it would be difficult to write literature that drew on just one of the four basic modes.

Exam Probability: **Medium**

22. Answer choices:

(see index for correct answer)

- a. Informal fallacy
- b. Fitch-style calculus
- c. Philosophical logic
- d. Description

Guidance: level 1

:: Logic ::

_____s are mental representations, abstract objects or abilities that make up the fundamental building blocks of thoughts and beliefs. They play an important role in all aspects of cognition.

Exam Probability: **Low**

23. Answer choices:

(see index for correct answer)

- a. Conditional quantifier
- b. Nonfirstorderizability
- c. Evolutionary logic
- d. Cotolerant sequence

Guidance: level 1

:: Programming paradigms ::

_____ is a programming paradigm, derived from structured programming, based upon the concept of the procedure call. Procedures, also known as routines, subroutines, or functions, simply contain a series of computational steps to be carried out. Any given procedure might be called at any point during a program's execution, including by other procedures or itself. The first major _____ languages first appeared circa 1960, including Fortran, ALGOL, COBOL and BASIC. Pascal and C were published closer to the 1970s.

Exam Probability: **Low**

24. *Answer choices:*

(see index for correct answer)

- a. object-oriented programming
- b. Procedural programming

Guidance: level 1

:: Transaction processing ::

Some scenarios associate "this kind of planning" with learning "life skills". _____ s are necessary, or at least useful, in situations where individuals need to know what time they must be at a specific location to receive a specific service, and where people need to accomplish a set of goals within a set time period.

Exam Probability: **Medium**

25. *Answer choices:*

(see index for correct answer)

- a. Extreme Transaction Processing
- b. Schedule
- c. Thomas write rule
- d. Long-running transaction

Guidance: level 1

:: Digital typography ::

_____ is a page description language in the electronic publishing and desktop publishing business. It is a dynamically typed, concatenative programming language and was created at Adobe Systems by John Warnock, Charles Geschke, Doug Brotz, Ed Taft and Bill Paxton from 1982 to 1984.

Exam Probability: **High**

26. *Answer choices:*

(see index for correct answer)

- a. OpenType
- b. Postscript
- c. Font Sense

- d. PostScript fonts

Guidance: level 1

:: Formal methods ::

_____ is the linguistic and philosophical study of meaning, in language, programming languages, formal logics, and semiotics. It is concerned with the relationship between signifiers—like words, phrases, signs, and symbols—and what they stand for in reality, their denotation.

Exam Probability: **Low**

27. *Answer choices:*
(see index for correct answer)

- a. Loop variant
- b. Semantics
- c. McCarthy 91 function
- d. Satisfiability Modulo Theories

Guidance: level 1

:: Pattern matching ::

In computer science, _____ is the act of checking a given sequence of tokens for the presence of the constituents of some pattern. In contrast to pattern recognition, the match usually has to be exact: "either it will or will not be a match." The patterns generally have the form of either sequences or tree structures. Uses of _____ include outputting the locations of a pattern within a token sequence, to output some component of the matched pattern, and to substitute the matching pattern with some other token sequence.

Exam Probability: **Medium**

28. *Answer choices:*

(see index for correct answer)

- a. Glob
- b. Wildmat
- c. RNA22
- d. Comparison of regular expression engines

Guidance: level 1

:: Mathematical logic ::

_____ is an arrangement and organization of interrelated elements in a material object or system, or the object or system so organized. Material _____ s include man-made objects such as buildings and machines and natural objects such as biological organisms, minerals and chemicals. Abstract _____ s include data _____ s in computer science and musical form. Types of _____ include a hierarchy , a network featuring many-to-many links, or a lattice featuring connections between components that are neighbors in space.

Exam Probability: **High**

29. *Answer choices:*

(see index for correct answer)

- a. Structure
- b. Conservativity theorem
- c. Beth definability
- d. Turnstile

Guidance: level 1

:: Data types ::

An _____ is a number that can be written without a fractional component. For example, 21, 4, 0, and -2048 are _____ s, while 9.75, 5 12, and 2 are not.

Exam Probability: **Medium**

30. Answer choices:

(see index for correct answer)

- a. Subtyping
- b. Opaque pointer
- c. Physical address
- d. Type rule

Guidance: level 1

:: OS X email clients ::

The _____ or post is a system for physically transporting postcards, letters, and parcels. A postal service can be private or public, though many governments place restrictions on private systems. Since the mid-19th century, national postal systems have generally been established as government monopolies, with a fee on the article prepaid. Proof of payment is often in the form of adhesive postage stamps, but postage meters are also used for bulk _____ing. Modern private postal systems are typically distinguished from national postal agencies by the names "courier" or "delivery service".

Exam Probability: **Low**

31. Answer choices:

(see index for correct answer)

- a. GroupWise
- b. Mail

- c. GyazMail

Guidance: level 1

:: Data types ::

The _____ is a unit of digital information that most commonly consists of eight bits, representing a binary number. Historically, the _____ was the number of bits used to encode a single character of text in a computer and for this reason it is the smallest addressable unit of memory in many computer architectures.

Exam Probability: **Low**

32. *Answer choices:*
(see index for correct answer)

- a. HRESULT
- b. Byte
- c. Algebraic data type
- d. Smart pointer

Guidance: level 1

:: Computing input devices ::

In computing, an _____ is a piece of computer hardware equipment used to provide data and control signals to an information processing system such as a computer or information appliance. Examples of _____ s include keyboards, mouse, scanners, digital cameras and joysticks. Audio _____ s may be used for purposes including speech recognition. Many companies are utilizing speech recognition to help assist users to use their device.

Exam Probability: **Medium**

33. *Answer choices:*

(see index for correct answer)

- a. Input device
- b. CueCat
- c. Touchatag
- d. Mir:ror

Guidance: level 1

:: Software testing ::

In computer programming, _____ is a software testing method by which individual units of source code, sets of one or more computer program modules together with associated control data, usage procedures, and operating procedures, are tested to determine whether they are fit for use.

Exam Probability: **Medium**

34. Answer choices:

(see index for correct answer)

- a. Regression testing
- b. Unit testing
- c. Daikon
- d. IEEE 829

Guidance: level 1

:: Central processing unit ::

A _____ , also called a central processor or main processor, is the electronic circuitry within a computer that carries out the instructions of a computer program by performing the basic arithmetic, logic, controlling, and input/output operations specified by the instructions. The computer industry has used the term " _____ " at least since the early 1960s. Traditionally, the term "CPU" refers to a processor, more specifically to its processing unit and control unit , distinguishing these core elements of a computer from external components such as main memory and I/O circuitry.

Exam Probability: **Medium**

35. Answer choices:

(see index for correct answer)

- a. Ring
- b. Register window

- c. Central processing unit
- d. Hardware register

Guidance: level 1

:: Data security ::

In computer science, _____ is the process of ensuring data have undergone data cleansing to ensure they have data quality, that is, that they are both correct and useful. It uses routines, often called "validation rules" "validation constraints" or "check routines", that check for correctness, meaningfulness, and security of data that are input to the system. The rules may be implemented through the automated facilities of a data dictionary, or by the inclusion of explicit application program validation logic.

Exam Probability: **High**

36. *Answer choices:*
(see index for correct answer)

- a. Password fatigue
- b. Data validation
- c. Certified Information Systems Auditor
- d. Sanitization

Guidance: level 1

:: Search algorithms ::

In computer science, a _____ is any algorithm which solves the search problem, namely, to retrieve information stored within some data structure, or calculated in the search space of a problem domain, either with discrete or continuous values. Specific applications of _____ s include.

Exam Probability: **High**

37. *Answer choices:*

(see index for correct answer)

- a. Search algorithm
- b. MaMF
- c. Beam search
- d. Linear search

Guidance: level 1

:: Formal languages ::

A _____ is a mark, sign or word that indicates, signifies, or is understood as representing an idea, object, or relationship. _____ s allow people to go beyond what is known or seen by creating linkages between otherwise very different concepts and experiences. All communication is achieved through the use of _____ s. _____ s take the form of words, sounds, gestures, ideas or visual images and are used to convey other ideas and beliefs. For example, a red octagon may be a _____ for "STOP". On a map, a blue line might represent a river. Numerals are _____ s for numbers. Alphabetic letters may be _____ s for sounds. Personal names are _____ s representing individuals. A red rose may _____ ize love and compassion. The variable `x`, in a mathematical equation, may _____ ize the position of a particle in space.

Exam Probability: **High**

38. *Answer choices:*

(see index for correct answer)

- a. Attribute grammar
- b. Definite clause grammar
- c. Symbol
- d. Top-down parsing language

Guidance: level 1

:: Virtual reality ::

Open Graphics Library is a cross-language, cross-platform application programming interface for rendering 2D and 3D vector graphics. The API is typically used to interact with a graphics processing unit, to achieve hardware-accelerated rendering.

Exam Probability: **Low**

39. *Answer choices:*

(see index for correct answer)

- a. Avizo
- b. Bump mapping
- c. OpenGL
- d. Free look

Guidance: level 1

:: Data structures ::

In computer science, a _____ is a tree data structure in which each node has at most two children, which are referred to as the left child and the right child. A recursive definition using just set theory notions is that a _____ is a tuple, where L and R are _____ s or the empty set and S is a singleton set. Some authors allow the _____ to be the empty set as well.

Exam Probability: **Medium**

40. Answer choices:

(see index for correct answer)

- a. Data structure
- b. Array data structure
- c. Linked data structure
- d. Retroactive data structures

Guidance: level 1

:: Prolog programming language family ::

_____ is a logic programming language associated with artificial intelligence and computational linguistics.

Exam Probability: **High**

41. Answer choices:

(see index for correct answer)

- a. SWI-Prolog
- b. JIProlog
- c. YAP
- d. Prolog

Guidance: level 1

:: Educational programming languages ::

A _____ is a physiological capacity of organisms that provides data for perception. The _____ s and their operation, classification, and theory are overlapping topics studied by a variety of fields, most notably neuroscience, cognitive psychology, and philosophy of perception. The nervous system has a specific sensory nervous system, and a _____ organ, or sensor, dedicated to each _____ .

Exam Probability: **Low**

42. *Answer choices:*

(see index for correct answer)

- a. Turing
- b. GNU MIX Development Kit
- c. Sense
- d. Microsoft Semblio

Guidance: level 1

:: Cryptography ::

In communications and information processing, _____ is a system of rules to convert information—such as a letter, word, sound, image, or gesture—into another form or representation, sometimes shortened or secret, for communication through a communication channel or storage in a storage medium. An early example is the invention of language, which enabled a person, through speech, to communicate what they saw, heard, felt, or thought to others. But speech limits the range of communication to the distance a voice can carry, and limits the audience to those present when the speech is uttered. The invention of writing, which converted spoken language into visual symbols, extended the range of communication across space and time.

Exam Probability: **Medium**

43. *Answer choices:*

(see index for correct answer)

- a. Cipher
- b. Diplomatic bag
- c. Tamper resistance
- d. Strong cryptography

Guidance: level 1

:: Planning ::

A _____ is a type of bar chart that illustrates a project schedule, named after its inventor, Henry Gantt, who designed such a chart around the years 1910–1915. Modern _____ s also show the dependency relationships between activities and current schedule status.

Exam Probability: **Medium**

44. *Answer choices:*

(see index for correct answer)

- a. Counterplan
- b. Succession planning
- c. Gantt chart
- d. BLUF

Guidance: level 1

:: Cluster computing ::

A _____ is a computer cluster of what are normally identical, commodity-grade computers networked into a small local area network with libraries and programs installed which allow processing to be shared among them. The result is a high-performance parallel computing cluster from inexpensive personal computer hardware.

Exam Probability: **High**

45. *Answer choices:*

(see index for correct answer)

- a. Moab Cluster Suite
- b. Beowulf cluster

- c. Project Kusu
- d. Rocks Cluster Distribution

Guidance: level 1

:: Identity ::

A _____ is a set of connected behaviors, rights, obligations, beliefs, and norms as conceptualized by people in a social situation. It is an expected or free or continuously changing behaviour and may have a given individual social status or social position. It is vital to both functionalist and interactionist understandings of society. Social _____ posits the following about social behaviour.

Exam Probability: **Low**

46. *Answer choices:*
(see index for correct answer)

- a. Law of identity
- b. Identity of indiscernibles
- c. Self-perception theory
- d. Role

Guidance: level 1

:: Operators (programming) ::

In programming, _____, sometimes termed operator ad hoc polymorphism, is a specific case of polymorphism, where different operators have different implementations depending on their arguments. _____ is generally defined by a programming language, a programmer, or both.

Exam Probability: **Low**

47. *Answer choices:*

(see index for correct answer)

- a. order of operation
- b. Operator overloading
- c. assignment statement
- d. decrement operators

Guidance: level 1

:: Artificial intelligence ::

In computer science, _____, sometimes called machine intelligence, is intelligence demonstrated by machines, in contrast to the natural intelligence displayed by humans and animals. Colloquially, the term "_____" is used to describe machines that mimic "cognitive" functions that humans associate with other human minds, such as "learning" and "problem solving".

Exam Probability: **High**

48. *Answer choices:*

(see index for correct answer)

- a. Ontology learning
- b. Artificial intelligence
- c. Neural modeling fields
- d. Color normalization

Guidance: level 1

:: Operators (programming) ::

In computer programming, an _____ sets and/or re-sets the value stored in the storage location denoted by a variable name; in other words, it copies a value into the variable. In most imperative programming languages, the _____ is a fundamental construct.

Exam Probability: **Medium**

49. *Answer choices:*

(see index for correct answer)

- a. decrement operators
- b. sizeof
- c. Dereference
- d. operator overloading

Guidance: level 1

:: Device drivers ::

In computing, a _____ is a computer program that operates or controls a particular type of device that is attached to a computer. A driver provides a software interface to hardware devices, enabling operating systems and other computer programs to access hardware functions without needing to know precise details about the hardware being used.

Exam Probability: **Low**

50. *Answer choices:*

(see index for correct answer)

- a. DOCS
- b. Kernel-Mode Driver Framework
- c. Universal Audio Architecture
- d. Device driver

Guidance: level 1

:: Distributed computing architecture ::

The _____ is a standard for distributed simulation, used when building a simulation for a larger purpose by combining several simulations. The standard was developed in the 90's under the leadership of the US Department of Defense and was later transitioned to become an open international IEEE standard. It is a recommended standard within NATO through STANAG 4603. Today the HLA is used in a number of domains including defense and security and civilian applications. The architecture specifies the following components.

Exam Probability: **Medium**

51. *Answer choices:*

(see index for correct answer)

- a. Distributed Interactive Simulation
- b. Distributed shared memory
- c. MapReduce
- d. High-level architecture

Guidance: level 1

:: Machine code ::

In computing, _____ or object module is the product of a compiler. In a general sense _____ is a sequence of statements or instructions in a computer language, usually a machine code language or an intermediate language such as register transfer language. The term indicates that the code is the goal or result of the compiling process, with some early sources referring to source code as a "subject program."

Exam Probability: **High**

52. *Answer choices:*

(see index for correct answer)

- a. Opcode
- b. Code generation
- c. Operand
- d. Object code

Guidance: level 1

:: Unified Modeling Language diagrams ::

In software engineering, a _____ in the Unified Modeling Language is a type of static structure diagram that describes the structure of a system by showing the system's classes, their attributes, operations, and the relationships among objects.

Exam Probability: **High**

53. *Answer choices:*

(see index for correct answer)

- a. Component diagram
- b. System sequence diagram
- c. Class diagram

- d. Timing diagram

Guidance: level 1

:: Algorithm description languages ::

_____ is an informal high-level description of the operating principle of a computer program or other algorithm.

Exam Probability: **Low**

54. *Answer choices:*

(see index for correct answer)

- a. Structured English
- b. Pseudocode
- c. Pidgin code
- d. PlusCal

Guidance: level 1

:: Client-server database management systems ::

_____ is an open-source relational database management system. Its name is a combination of "My", the name of co-founder Michael Widenius's daughter, and "SQL", the abbreviation for Structured Query Language.

Exam Probability: **Low**

55. *Answer choices:*

(see index for correct answer)

- a. MySQL
- b. PostgreSQL
- c. Transbase

Guidance: level 1

:: Sorting algorithms ::

_____ is a simple sorting algorithm that builds the final sorted array one item at a time. It is much less efficient on large lists than more advanced algorithms such as quicksort, heapsort, or merge sort. However, _____ provides several advantages.

Exam Probability: **Low**

56. *Answer choices:*

(see index for correct answer)

- a. Cartesian tree
- b. Pairwise sorting network
- c. Bogosort
- d. Cocktail sort

Guidance: level 1

:: Functional programming ::

In computer science, _____ is a programming paradigm—a style of building the structure and elements of computer programs—that treats computation as the evaluation of mathematical functions and avoids changing-state and mutable data. It is a declarative programming paradigm in that programming is done with expressions or declarations instead of statements. Functional code is idempotent: a function's return value depends only on its arguments, so calling a function with the same value for an argument always produces the same result. This is in contrast to imperative programming where, in addition to a function's arguments, global program state can affect a function's resulting value. Eliminating side effects, that is, changes in state that do not depend on the function inputs, can make understanding a program easier, which is one of the key motivations for the development of _____ .

Exam Probability: **Medium**

57. *Answer choices:*
(see index for correct answer)

- a. mutable
- b. Functional programming

Guidance: level 1

:: Metadata ::

An _____ is a name that identifies either a unique object or a unique class of objects, where the "object" or class may be an idea, physical [countable] object, or physical [noncountable] substance. The abbreviation ID often refers to identity, identification, or an _____. An _____ may be a word, number, letter, symbol, or any combination of those.

Exam Probability: **Medium**

58. *Answer choices:*

(see index for correct answer)

- a. Uniform Type Identifier
- b. Creator ID
- c. E-GMS
- d. Data element definition

Guidance: level 1

:: Data structures ::

In computer science, _____ means that a group of elements is accessed in a predetermined, ordered sequence. _____ is sometimes the only way of accessing the data, for example if it is on a tape. It may also be the access method of choice, for example if all that is wanted is to process a sequence of data elements in order.

Exam Probability: **Low**

59. *Answer choices:*

(see index for correct answer)

- a. Linked data structure
- b. Spaghetti stack
- c. Sequential access
- d. Disjoint-set data structure

Guidance: level 1

Computer security

Computer security, cybersecurity or information technology security (IT security) is the protection of computer systems from theft or damage to their hardware, software or electronic data, as well as from disruption or misdirection of the services they provide.

:: Cryptography ::

In communications and information processing, _____ is a system of rules to convert information—such as a letter, word, sound, image, or gesture—into another form or representation, sometimes shortened or secret, for communication through a communication channel or storage in a storage medium. An early example is the invention of language, which enabled a person, through speech, to communicate what they saw, heard, felt, or thought to others. But speech limits the range of communication to the distance a voice can carry, and limits the audience to those present when the speech is uttered. The invention of writing, which converted spoken language into visual symbols, extended the range of communication across space and time.

Exam Probability: **Low**

1. *Answer choices:*

(see index for correct answer)

- a. Decipherment
- b. Snake oil
- c. Code
- d. CryptoParty

Guidance: level 1

:: Cryptography ::

_____ happens whenever a system that is designed to be closed to an eavesdropper reveals some information to unauthorized parties nonetheless. For example, when designing an encrypted instant messaging network, a network engineer without the capacity to crack encryption codes could see when messages are transmitted, even if he could not read them. During the Second World War, the Japanese for a while were using secret codes such as PURPLE; even before such codes were cracked, some basic information could be extracted about the content of the messages by looking at which relay stations sent a message onward. As another example of _____, GPU drivers do not erase their memories and thus, in shared/local/global memories, data values persist after deallocation. These data can be retrieved by a malicious agent.

Exam Probability: **High**

2. *Answer choices:*

(see index for correct answer)

- a. Encrypted function
- b. Cryptochannel
- c. Symmetric Boolean function
- d. CRIME

Guidance: level 1

:: Application layer protocols ::

The _____ is a network management protocol used on UDP/IP networks whereby a DHCP server dynamically assigns an IP address and other network configuration parameters to each device on a network so they can communicate with other IP networks. A DHCP server enables computers to request IP addresses and networking parameters automatically from the Internet service provider, reducing the need for a network administrator or a user to manually assign IP addresses to all network devices. In the absence of a DHCP server, a computer or other device on the network needs to be manually assigned an IP address, or to assign itself an APIPA address, which will not enable it to communicate outside its local subnet.

Exam Probability: **Low**

3. *Answer choices:*

(see index for correct answer)

- a. RadSec
- b. Dynamic Host Configuration Protocol
- c. MMS Architecture
- d. Inter-Asterisk eXchange

Guidance: level 1

:: Computer network security ::

A _____ is an application which controls network traffic to and from a computer, permitting or denying communications based on a security policy. Typically it works as an application layer firewall.

Exam Probability: **Low**

4. *Answer choices:*

(see index for correct answer)

- a. Anti-worm
- b. Juniper Networks
- c. Forward-confirmed reverse DNS
- d. Null session

Guidance: level 1

:: Business continuity and disaster recovery ::

In information technology, a _____ , or data _____ , or the process of backing up, refers to the copying into an archive file of computer data that is already in secondary storage—so that it may be used to restore the original after a data loss event. The verb form is "back up", whereas the noun and adjective form is " _____ ".

Exam Probability: **Medium**

5. *Answer choices:*

(see index for correct answer)

- a. VirtualSharp Software
- b. Disaster Recovery Advisor

- c. Granular configuration automation
- d. Backup Express

Guidance: level 1

:: Computer network security ::

A _____ is a number of Internet-connected devices, each of which is running one or more bots. _____ s can be used to perform distributed denial-of-service attack, steal data, send spam, and allows the attacker to access the device and its connection. The owner can control the _____ using command and control software. The word " _____ " is a combination of the words "robot" and "network". The term is usually used with a negative or malicious connotation.

Exam Probability: **Medium**

6. *Answer choices:*

(see index for correct answer)

- a. Cryptek
- b. Application-level gateway
- c. Botnet
- d. Password length parameter

Guidance: level 1

:: Measurement ::

_____ is a property that can exist as a multitude or magnitude. Quantities can be compared in terms of "more", "less", or "equal", or by assigning a numerical value in terms of a unit of measurement. _____ is among the basic classes of things along with quality, substance, change, and relation. Some quantities are such by their inner nature , while others are functioning as states of things such as heavy and light, long and short, broad and narrow, small and great, or much and little.

Exam Probability: **Medium**

7. *Answer choices:*

(see index for correct answer)

- a. Sampling error
- b. Quantity
- c. Colorimetry
- d. Berkson error model

Guidance: level 1

:: Computer network security ::

An _____ is a controlled private network that allows access to partners, vendors and suppliers or an authorized set of customers – normally to a subset of the information accessible from an organization's intranet. An _____ is similar to a DMZ in that it provides access to needed services for authorized parties, without granting access to an organization's entire network. An _____ is a private network organization.

Exam Probability: **Low**

8. *Answer choices:*

(see index for correct answer)

- a. Cutwail botnet
- b. Ticket
- c. Sybil attack
- d. Extranet

Guidance: level 1

:: Cryptography ::

_____ is a technology developed and promoted by the _____ Group. The term is taken from the field of trusted systems and has a specialized meaning. With _____, the computer will consistently behave in expected ways, and those behaviors will be enforced by computer hardware and software. Enforcing this behavior is achieved by loading the hardware with a unique encryption key inaccessible to the rest of the system.

Exam Probability: **High**

9. *Answer choices:*

(see index for correct answer)

- a. Strong cryptography
- b. BREACH
- c. Functional encryption
- d. Codebook

Guidance: level 1

:: Data analysis ::

_____ is the process of discovering patterns in large data sets involving methods at the intersection of machine learning, statistics, and database systems. _____ is an interdisciplinary subfield of computer science and statistics with an overall goal to extract information from a data set and transform the information into a comprehensible structure for further use. _____ is the analysis step of the "knowledge discovery in databases" process, or KDD. Aside from the raw analysis step, it also involves database and data management aspects, data pre-processing, model and inference considerations, interestingness metrics, complexity considerations, post-processing of discovered structures, visualization, and online updating. The difference between data analysis and _____ is that data analysis is used to test models and hypotheses on the dataset, e.g., analyzing the effectiveness of a marketing campaign, regardless of the amount of data; in contrast, _____ uses machine-learning and statistical models to uncover clandestine or hidden patterns in a large volume of data.

Exam Probability: **Medium**

10. *Answer choices:*

(see index for correct answer)

- a. Explained variation
- b. Window function
- c. Covariance matrix
- d. Data mining

Guidance: level 1

:: Cryptographic attacks ::

In cryptography, a _____ consists of an attacker submitting many passwords or passphrases with the hope of eventually guessing correctly. The attacker systematically checks all possible passwords and passphrases until the correct one is found. Alternatively, the attacker can attempt to guess the key which is typically created from the password using a key derivation function. This is known as an exhaustive key search.

Exam Probability: **Low**

11. *Answer choices:*

(see index for correct answer)

- a. Linear cryptanalysis
- b. Distinguishing attack

- c. Brute-force attack
- d. Boomerang attack

Guidance: level 1

:: File sharing networks ::

_____ computing or networking is a distributed application architecture that partitions tasks or workloads between peers. Peers are equally privileged, equipotent participants in the application. They are said to form a _____ network of nodes.

Exam Probability: **Medium**

12. *Answer choices:*

(see index for correct answer)

- a. Peer-to-peer
- b. Open Media Network
- c. Multisource File Transfer Protocol
- d. EDonkey network

Guidance: level 1

:: World Wide Web ::

_____ LLC is an American multinational technology company that specializes in Internet-related services and products, which include online advertising technologies, search engine, cloud computing, software, and hardware. It is considered one of the Big Four technology companies, alongside Amazon, Apple and Facebook.

Exam Probability: **High**

13. *Answer choices:*

(see index for correct answer)

- a. Page hijacking
- b. Google
- c. Server Side Includes
- d. E-patient

Guidance: level 1

:: Malware ::

In distributed computing, code mobility is the ability for running programs, code or objects to be migrated from one machine or application to another. This is the process of moving _____ across the nodes of a network as opposed to distributed computation where the data is moved.

Exam Probability: **High**

14. *Answer choices:*

(see index for correct answer)

- a. Shnakule
- b. MonaRonaDona
- c. Riskware
- d. Stealware

Guidance: level 1

:: Computer security ::

_____ refers to a situation where a statement's author cannot successfully dispute its authorship or the validity of an associated contract. The term is often seen in a legal setting when the authenticity of a signature is being challenged. In such an instance, the authenticity is being "repudiated".

Exam Probability: **Low**

15. *Answer choices:*

(see index for correct answer)

- a. Stepping stone
- b. Centurion guard
- c. IEC 60870-6
- d. Non-repudiation

Guidance: level 1

:: Information technology organisations ::

_____ is a non-profit organization serving as a public-private partnership between U.S. businesses and the Federal Bureau of Investigation. The organization is an information sharing and analysis effort serving the interests, and combining the knowledge base of, a wide range of private sector and government members. _____ is an association of individuals that facilitates information sharing and intelligence between businesses, academic institutions, state and local law enforcement agencies, and other participants dedicated to prevent hostile acts against the United States. _____'s mutual nondisclosure agreements among its members and the FBI promotes trusted discussions of vulnerabilities and solutions that companies and individuals may be hesitant to place in the public domain and provide access to additional threat information from the FBI.

Exam Probability: **Low**

16. *Answer choices:*
(see index for correct answer)

- a. Girl Geeks Scotland
- b. Logic Programming Associates
- c. Netskills
- d. InfraGard

Guidance: level 1

:: Data transmission ::

In telecommunication a _____ is the means of connecting one location to another for the purpose of transmitting and receiving digital information. It can also refer to a set of electronics assemblies, consisting of a transmitter and a receiver and the interconnecting data telecommunication circuit. These are governed by a link protocol enabling digital data to be transferred from a data source to a data sink.

Exam Probability: **High**

17. *Answer choices:*

(see index for correct answer)

- a. Variable bitrate
- b. Degree of isochronous distortion
- c. Parallel communication
- d. Data link

Guidance: level 1

:: Computer security models ::

_____ or multiple levels of security is the application of a computer system to process information with incompatible classifications, permit access by users with different security clearances and needs-to-know, and prevent users from obtaining access to information for which they lack authorization. There are two contexts for the use of _____ . One is to refer to a system that is adequate to protect itself from subversion and has robust mechanisms to separate information domains, that is, trustworthy. Another context is to refer to an application of a computer that will require the computer to be strong enough to protect itself from subversion and possess adequate mechanisms to separate information domains, that is, a system we must trust. This distinction is important because systems that need to be trusted are not necessarily trustworthy.

Exam Probability: **High**

18. *Answer choices:*

(see index for correct answer)

- a. Computer security policy
- b. HRU
- c. Multilevel security
- d. Non-interference

Guidance: level 1

:: Application layer protocols ::

A _____ is a set of algorithms that help secure a network connection that uses Transport Layer Security or its now-deprecated predecessor Secure Socket Layer . The set of algorithms that _____ s usually contain include: a key exchange algorithm, a bulk encryption algorithm, and a message authentication code algorithm.

Exam Probability: **Low**

19. *Answer choices:*

(see index for correct answer)

- a. Media Resource Control Protocol
- b. Cipher suite
- c. File Access Listener
- d. Service discovery

Guidance: level 1

:: Cryptographic attacks ::

In cryptanalysis and computer security, a _____ is a form of brute force attack technique for defeating a cipher or authentication mechanism by trying to determine its decryption key or passphrase by trying hundreds or sometimes millions of likely possibilities, such as words in a dictionary.

Exam Probability: **High**

20. Answer choices:

(see index for correct answer)

- a. Dictionary attack
- b. Message forgery
- c. Meet-in-the-middle attack
- d. Truncated differential cryptanalysis

Guidance: level 1

:: Internet governance organizations ::

The _____ is the coordination center of the computer emergency response team for the Software Engineering Institute, a non-profit United States federally funded research and development center. The CERT/CC researches software bugs that impact software and internet security, publishes research and information on its findings, and works with business and government to improve security of software and the internet as a whole.

Exam Probability: **High**

21. Answer choices:

(see index for correct answer)

- a. CERT Coordination Center
- b. PICISOC
- c. InternetNZ
- d. Internet Technical Committee

Guidance: level 1

:: Cryptography ::

The Secure Hash Algorithms are a family of cryptographic hash functions published by the National Institute of Standards and Technology as a U.S. Federal Information Processing Standard, including.

Exam Probability: **Low**

22. *Answer choices:*

(see index for correct answer)

- a. Verifiable secret sharing
- b. Secure Hash Standard
- c. WYSIWYS
- d. Deniable encryption

Guidance: level 1

:: Spamming ::

_____ is the fraudulent attempt to obtain sensitive information such as usernames, passwords and credit card details by disguising oneself as a trustworthy entity in an electronic communication. Typically carried out by email spoofing or instant messaging, it often directs users to enter personal information at a fake website which matches the look and feel of the legitimate site.

Exam Probability: **High**

23. *Answer choices:*

(see index for correct answer)

- a. Spam 2.0
- b. Keyword stuffing
- c. Phishing
- d. Link farm

Guidance: level 1

:: Data privacy ::

The _____ is an information security standard for organizations that handle branded credit cards from the major card schemes.

Exam Probability: **Low**

24. *Answer choices:*

(see index for correct answer)

- a. Quasi-identifier
- b. Health Insurance Portability and Accountability Act
- c. Payment Card Industry Data Security Standard
- d. Danish Data Protection Agency

Guidance: level 1

:: Security compliance ::

_____ refers to the inability to withstand the effects of a hostile environment. A window of _____ is a time frame within which defensive measures are diminished, compromised or lacking.

Exam Probability: **High**

25. *Answer choices:*

(see index for correct answer)

- a. North American Electric Reliability Corporation
- b. 201 CMR 17.00

Guidance: level 1

:: Internet security ::

_____ , and its now-deprecated predecessor, Secure Sockets Layer , are cryptographic protocols designed to provide communications security over a computer network. Several versions of the protocols find widespread use in applications such as web browsing, email, instant messaging, and voice over IP . Websites can use TLS to secure all communications between their servers and web browsers.

Exam Probability: **Low**

26. *Answer choices:*

(see index for correct answer)

- a. Internet censorship circumvention
- b. DNSChanger
- c. Mastering the Internet
- d. Internet security

Guidance: level 1

:: Malware ::

A _____ is a piece of code intentionally inserted into a software system that will set off a malicious function when specified conditions are met. For example, a programmer may hide a piece of code that starts deleting files , should they ever be terminated from the company.

Exam Probability: **Medium**

27. Answer choices:

(see index for correct answer)

- a. Browser hijacking
- b. Micro Bill Systems
- c. Shnakule
- d. Logic bomb

Guidance: level 1

:: Deep packet inspection ::

_____, Inc. is an American multinational technology conglomerate headquartered in San Jose, California, in the center of Silicon Valley. Cisco develops, manufactures and sells networking hardware, telecommunications equipment and other high-technology services and products. Through its numerous acquired subsidiaries, such as OpenDNS, WebEx, Jabber and Jasper, Cisco specializes into specific tech markets, such as Internet of Things , domain security and energy management.

Exam Probability: **Medium**

28. Answer choices:

(see index for correct answer)

- a. Radware
- b. Front Porch
- c. Procera Networks

- d. Sandvine

Guidance: level 1

:: Revision control systems ::

_____ is a systems engineering process for establishing and maintaining consistency of a product's performance, functional, and physical attributes with its requirements, design, and operational information throughout its life. The CM process is widely used by military engineering organizations to manage changes throughout the system lifecycle of complex systems, such as weapon systems, military vehicles, and information systems. Outside the military, the CM process is also used with IT service management as defined by ITIL, and with other domain models in the civil engineering and other industrial engineering segments such as roads, bridges, canals, dams, and buildings.

Exam Probability: **High**

29. *Answer choices:*

(see index for correct answer)

- a. Baseline
- b. CVSNT
- c. Autodesk Vault
- d. Configuration management

Guidance: level 1

:: Internet privacy ::

_____ is when two entities are communicating and do not want a third party to listen in. For that they need to communicate in a way not susceptible to eavesdropping or interception. _____ includes means by which people can share information with varying degrees of certainty that third parties cannot intercept what was said. Other than spoken face-to-face communication with no possible eavesdropper, it is probably safe to say that no communication is guaranteed secure in this sense, although practical obstacles such as legislation, resources, technical issues, and the sheer volume of communication serve to limit surveillance.

Exam Probability: **Low**

30. *Answer choices:*

(see index for correct answer)

- a. Geolocation software
- b. Secure communication
- c. Freegate
- d. CSipSimple

Guidance: level 1

:: Cryptographic protocols ::

_____ is any method in cryptography by which cryptographic keys are exchanged between two parties, allowing use of a cryptographic algorithm.

Exam Probability: **High**

31. *Answer choices:*

(see index for correct answer)

- a. Chaffing and winnowing
- b. Security protocol
- c. Homomorphic secret sharing
- d. Key exchange

Guidance: level 1

:: Information technology qualifications ::

The Computing Technology Industry Association , is a non-profit trade association, issuing professional certifications for the information technology industry. It is considered one of the IT industry's top trade associations. Based in Downers Grove, Illinois, _____ issues vendor-neutral professional certifications in over 120 countries. The organization releases over 50 industry studies annually to track industry trends and changes. Over 2.2 million people have earned _____ certifications since the association was established.

Exam Probability: **Medium**

32. *Answer choices:*

(see index for correct answer)

- a. Cisco Career Certifications
- b. IC3
- c. Certified Social Engineering Prevention Specialist
- d. Diploma in Digital Applications

Guidance: level 1

:: Computer access control ::

In computer security, _____ is a type of access control defined by the Trusted Computer System Evaluation Criteria "as a means of restricting access to objects based on the identity of subjects and/or groups to which they belong. The controls are discretionary in the sense that a subject with a certain access permission is capable of passing that permission on to any other subject ".

Exam Probability: **Medium**

33. *Answer choices:*

(see index for correct answer)

- a. Context-based access control
- b. Time-based One-time Password Algorithm
- c. Discretionary access control
- d. Voms

Guidance: level 1

:: Computer network security ::

_____ is a security algorithm for IEEE 802.11 wireless networks. Introduced as part of the original 802.11 standard ratified in 1997, its intention was to provide data confidentiality comparable to that of a traditional wired network. WEP, recognizable by its key of 10 or 26 hexadecimal digits , was at one time widely in use and was often the first security choice presented to users by router configuration tools.

Exam Probability: **Low**

34. *Answer choices:*

(see index for correct answer)

- a. Robust random early detection
- b. Wired Equivalent Privacy
- c. OpenConnect
- d. SecureWorks

Guidance: level 1

:: Hacking (computer security) ::

The _____ is a United States cybersecurity bill that was enacted in 1984 as an amendment to existing computer fraud law, which had been included in the Comprehensive Crime Control Act of 1984. The law prohibits accessing a computer without authorization, or in excess of authorization. Prior to computer-specific criminal laws, computer crimes were prosecuted as mail and wire fraud, but the applying law was often insufficient.

Exam Probability: **High**

35. *Answer choices:*

(see index for correct answer)

- a. Firesheep
- b. Computer Fraud and Abuse Act
- c. RF monitor software
- d. Network detector

Guidance: level 1

:: Computer access control protocols ::

An _____ is a type of computer communications protocol or cryptographic protocol specifically designed for transfer of authentication data between two entities. It allows the receiving entity to authenticate the connecting entity as well as authenticate itself to the connecting entity by declaring the type of information needed for authentication as well as syntax. It is the most important layer of protection needed for secure communication within computer networks.

Exam Probability: **Medium**

36. *Answer choices:*

(see index for correct answer)

- a. Extensible Authentication Protocol
- b. NTLMSSP
- c. Authentication protocol
- d. Yahalom

Guidance: level 1

:: Computer security exploits ::

A single wardialing call would involve calling an unknown number, and waiting for one or two rings, since answering computers usually pick up on the first ring. If the phone rings twice, the modem hangs up and tries the next number. If a modem or fax machine answers, the wardialer program makes a note of the number. If a human or answering machine answers, the wardialer program hangs up. Depending on the time of day, wardialing 10,000 numbers in a given area code might annoy dozens or hundreds of people, some who attempt and fail to answer a phone in two rings, and some who succeed, only to hear the wardialing modem's carrier tone and hang up. The repeated incoming calls are especially annoying to businesses that have many consecutively numbered lines in the exchange, such as used with a Centrex telephone system.

Exam Probability: **High**

37. *Answer choices:*

(see index for correct answer)

- a. Virus hoax
- b. Email injection
- c. Windows Metafile vulnerability
- d. Exploit

Guidance: level 1

:: Computer security ::

_____ is the technique used for gathering information about computer systems and the entities they belong to. To get this information, a hacker might use various tools and technologies. This information is very useful to a hacker who is trying to crack a whole system.

Exam Probability: **High**

38. *Answer choices:*
(see index for correct answer)

- a. Information security
- b. Enterprise information security architecture
- c. Simple Certificate Enrollment Protocol
- d. Vulnerability Discovery Model

Guidance: level 1

:: Network analyzers ::

An _____ is a race of bestial spider-men aberrations in the Dungeons & Dragons fantasy roleplaying game.

Exam Probability: **High**

39. *Answer choices:*

(see index for correct answer)

- a. Network weathermap
- b. Ettercap
- c. DSniff
- d. Audit Record Generation and Utilization System

Guidance: level 1

:: Network analyzers ::

In computer networking, _____ is a mode for a wired network interface controller or wireless network interface controller that causes the controller to pass all traffic it receives to the central processing unit rather than passing only the frames that the controller is specifically programmed to receive. This mode is normally used for packet sniffing that takes place on a router or on a computer connected to a wired network or one being part of a wireless LAN. Interfaces are placed into _____ by software bridges often used with hardware virtualization.

Exam Probability: **Low**

40. *Answer choices:*

(see index for correct answer)

- a. NeDi
- b. Openkore
- c. Plink
- d. SNMPTT

Guidance: level 1

:: Computer network security ::

In cryptography, a _____ is part of a cryptosystem intended to reduce the risks inherent in exchanging keys. KDCs often operate in systems within which some users may have permission to use certain services at some times and not at others.

Exam Probability: **Low**

41. *Answer choices:*

(see index for correct answer)

- a. Key distribution center
- b. Festi botnet
- c. Fortinet
- d. Lethic botnet

Guidance: level 1

:: Computer network security ::

A demilitarized zone, _____ or DZ is an area in which treaties or agreements between nations, military powers or contending groups forbid military installations, activities or personnel. A _____ often lies along an established frontier or boundary between two or more military powers or alliances. A _____ may sometimes form a de facto international border, such as the 38th parallel between North and South Korea. Other examples of demilitarized zones are a 120-mile wide area between Iraq and Kuwait, Antarctica and outer space.

Exam Probability: **Low**

42. *Answer choices:*

(see index for correct answer)

- a. DMZ
- b. BartVPN
- c. Metulji botnet
- d. Service scan

Guidance: level 1

:: Computer network security ::

A _____ extends a private network across a public network, and enables users to send and receive data across shared or public networks as if their computing devices were directly connected to the private network. Applications running on a computing device, e.g. a laptop, desktop, smartphone, across a VPN may therefore benefit from the functionality, security, and management of the private network. Encryption is a common though not an inherent part of a VPN connection.

Exam Probability: **Medium**

43. *Answer choices:*
(see index for correct answer)

- a. Virtual private network
- b. Clarified Networks
- c. Ticket
- d. Microsoft SmartScreen

Guidance: level 1

:: Mereology ::

_____ , in the abstract, is what belongs to or with something, whether as an attribute or as a component of said thing. In the context of this article, it is one or more components , whether physical or incorporeal, of a person's estate; or so belonging to, as in being owned by, a person or jointly a group of people or a legal entity like a corporation or even a society. Depending on the nature of the _____ , an owner of _____ has the right to consume, alter, share, redefine, rent, mortgage, pawn, sell, exchange, transfer, give away or destroy it, or to exclude others from doing these things, as well as to perhaps abandon it; whereas regardless of the nature of the _____ , the owner thereof has the right to properly use it , or at the very least exclusively keep it.

Exam Probability: **High**

44. *Answer choices:*
(see index for correct answer)

- a. Mereological essentialism
- b. Mereological nihilism
- c. Non-wellfounded mereology
- d. Mereology

Guidance: level 1

:: Data security ::

ISACA is an international professional association focused on IT governance. On its IRS filings, it is known as the Information Systems Audit and Control Association, although ISACA now goes by its acronym only.

Exam Probability: **Medium**

45. *Answer choices:*

(see index for correct answer)

- a. Self-destruct
- b. Jericho Forum Commandments
- c. Certified Information Systems Auditor
- d. Backup validation

Guidance: level 1

:: Computer security exploits ::

_____ is a type of computer security vulnerability typically found in web applications. XSS enables attackers to inject client-side scripts into web pages viewed by other users. A _____ vulnerability may be used by attackers to bypass access controls such as the same-origin policy. _____ carried out on websites accounted for roughly 84% of all security vulnerabilities documented by Symantec as of 2007. In 2017, XSS was still considered a major threat vector. XSS effects vary in range from petty nuisance to significant security risk, depending on the sensitivity of the data handled by the vulnerable site and the nature of any security mitigation implemented by the site's owner.

Exam Probability: **High**

46. *Answer choices:*

(see index for correct answer)

- a. Reflection attack
- b. Cross-site scripting
- c. TCP reset attack
- d. Virtual machine escape

Guidance: level 1

:: Computer security procedures ::

_____ is the identification of an organization's assets, followed by the development, documentation, and implementation of policies and procedures for protecting these assets.

Exam Probability: **Low**

47. *Answer choices:*

(see index for correct answer)

- a. MyNetWatchman
- b. Need to know
- c. CBL Index
- d. Full disclosure

Guidance: level 1

:: Computer network security ::

In cryptography and computer security, a _____ is an attack where the attacker secretly relays and possibly alters the communications between two parties who believe they are directly communicating with each other. One example of a MITM attack is active eavesdropping, in which the attacker makes independent connections with the victims and relays messages between them to make them believe they are talking directly to each other over a private connection, when in fact the entire conversation is controlled by the attacker. The attacker must be able to intercept all relevant messages passing between the two victims and inject new ones. This is straightforward in many circumstances; for example, an attacker within reception range of an unencrypted wireless access point could insert themselves as a man-in-the-middle.

Exam Probability: **Low**

48. *Answer choices:*

(see index for correct answer)

- a. Man-in-the-middle attack
- b. Cisco PIX
- c. 360 Safeguard
- d. Anti-worm

Guidance: level 1

:: Computer access control ::

_____ is the act of confirming the truth of an attribute of a single piece of data claimed true by an entity. In contrast with identification, which refers to the act of stating or otherwise indicating a claim purportedly attesting to a person or thing's identity, _____ is the process of actually confirming that identity. It might involve confirming the identity of a person by validating their identity documents, verifying the authenticity of a website with a digital certificate, determining the age of an artifact by carbon dating, or ensuring that a product is what its packaging and labeling claim to be. In other words, _____ often involves verifying the validity of at least one form of identification.

Exam Probability: **Low**

49. *Answer choices:*

(see index for correct answer)

- a. Single sign-on
- b. Authentication
- c. Java Authentication and Authorization Service
- d. Delegated administration

Guidance: level 1

:: Microsoft Windows file system technology ::

The _____ on Microsoft Windows is a feature introduced in version 3.0 of NTFS that provides filesystem-level encryption. The technology enables files to be transparently encrypted to protect confidential data from attackers with physical access to the computer.

Exam Probability: **Medium**

50. *Answer choices:*

(see index for correct answer)

- a. Encrypting File System
- b. Drive mapping
- c. Microsoft ScanDisk
- d. Diskcopy

Guidance: level 1

:: Order theory ::

_____ is an e-commerce payment system used in the Netherlands, based on online banking. Introduced in 2005, this payment method allows customers to buy on the Internet using direct online transfers from their bank account.

Exam Probability: **High**

51. *Answer choices:*

(see index for correct answer)

- a. Complete partial order
- b. Lexicographical order
- c. IDEAL
- d. Aronszajn line

Guidance: level 1

:: Cryptography ::

_____ is a security exploit against secret web cookies over connections using the HTTPS and SPDY protocols that also use data compression. When used to recover the content of secret authentication cookies, it allows an attacker to perform session hijacking on an authenticated web session, allowing the launching of further attacks. _____ was assigned CVE-2012-4929.

Exam Probability: **Low**

52. *Answer choices:*

(see index for correct answer)

- a. Vormetric
- b. CRIME
- c. Pizzino
- d. Plaintext

Guidance: level 1

:: Cryptography ::

In the mathematics of the real numbers, the logarithm logb a is a number x such that bx = a, for given numbers a and b. Analogously, in any group G, powers bk can be defined for all integers k, and the _____ logb a is an integer k such that bk = a. In number theory, the more commonly used term is index: we can write x = indr a   for rx = a   if r is a primitive root of m and gcd = 1.

Exam Probability: **Medium**

53. *Answer choices:*

(see index for correct answer)

- a. Electronic signature
- b. Friend-to-friend
- c. Discrete logarithm
- d. Key

Guidance: level 1

:: Data security ::

In 1991, John McCumber created a model framework for establishing and evaluating information security programs, now known as The _____ .This security model is depicted as a three-dimensional Rubik's Cube-like grid.

Exam Probability: **High**

54. *Answer choices:*

(see index for correct answer)

- a. Holistic Information Security Practitioner
- b. McCumber cube
- c. Information repository
- d. Federation Against Software Theft

Guidance: level 1

:: Computer security exploits ::

In cryptanalysis and computer security, _____ is the process of recovering passwords from data that have been stored in or transmitted by a computer system. A common approach is to try guesses repeatedly for the password and check them against an available cryptographic hash of the password.

Exam Probability: **High**

55. *Answer choices:*

(see index for correct answer)

- a. Replay attack
- b. SMBRelay

- c. Racetrack problem
- d. JIT spraying

Guidance: level 1

:: Computer security ::

A _____ is a communicated intent to inflict harm or loss on another person. A _____ is considered an act of coercion. _____ s are widely observed in animal behavior, particularly in a ritualized form, chiefly in order to avoid the unnecessary physical violence that can lead to physical damage or the death of both conflicting parties.

Exam Probability: **Low**

56. *Answer choices:*

(see index for correct answer)

- a. Security Token Service
- b. Threat
- c. VPN blocking
- d. Standard of Good Practice

Guidance: level 1

:: Mathematical structures ::

_____ s serve several societal needs – primarily as shelter from weather, security, living space, privacy, to store belongings, and to comfortably live and work. A _____ as a shelter represents a physical division of the human habitat and the outside .

Exam Probability: **Low**

57. *Answer choices:*

(see index for correct answer)

- a. Prosolvable group
- b. Periodic matrix set
- c. Building
- d. Algebraic structure

Guidance: level 1

:: Computer security exploits ::

In computer security, a _____ is a type of attack that creates a capability to transfer information objects between processes that are not supposed to be allowed to communicate by the computer security policy. The term, originated in 1973 by Lampson, is defined as channels "not intended for information transfer at all, such as the service program's effect on system load," to distinguish it from legitimate channels that are subjected to access controls by COMPUSEC.

Exam Probability: **Medium**

58. *Answer choices:*

(see index for correct answer)

- a. Heap feng shui
- b. Covert channel
- c. Reflected DOM Injection
- d. Shatter attack

Guidance: level 1

:: Internet protocols ::

In geometry, a _____ of a circle is any straight line segment that passes through the center of the circle and whose endpoints lie on the circle. It can also be defined as the longest chord of the circle. Both definitions are also valid for the _____ of a sphere.

Exam Probability: **Low**

59. *Answer choices:*

(see index for correct answer)

- a. Diameter
- b. Common Indexing Protocol
- c. SDES
- d. MS-CHAP

Guidance: level 1

Theoretical computer science

Theoretical computer science is a subset of general computer science and mathematics that focuses on more mathematical topics of computing and includes the theory of computation. While logical it is inference and mathematical proof had existed previously, in 1931 Kurt Gödel proved with his incompleteness theorem that there are fundamental limitations on what statements could be proved or disproved. These developments have led to the modern study of logic and computability, and indeed the field of theoretical computer science as a whole

:: Logic in computer science ::

_____ is a notation to eliminate the need for quantified variables in mathematical logic. It was introduced by Moses Schönfinkel and Haskell Curry, and has more recently been used in computer science as a theoretical model of computation and also as a basis for the design of functional programming languages. It is based on combinators which were introduced by Schönfinkel in 1920 with the idea of providing an analogous way to build up functions - and to remove any mention of variables - particularly in predicate logic. A combinator is a higher-order function that uses only function application and earlier defined combinators to define a result from its arguments.

Exam Probability: **High**

1. *Answer choices:*

(see index for correct answer)

- a. Operational semantics
- b. Combinatory logic
- c. Unification
- d. Denotational semantics

Guidance: level 1

:: Wavelets ::

In the mathematical topic of wavelet theory, the _____ is a numerical method for calculating function values of the basic scaling and wavelet functions of a discrete wavelet transform using an iterative algorithm. It starts from values on a coarse sequence of sampling points and produces values for successively more densely spaced sequences of sampling points. Because it applies the same operation over and over to the output of the previous application, it is known as the _____ .

Exam Probability: **High**

2. *Answer choices:*

(see index for correct answer)

- a. Dynamic link matching
- b. Lifting scheme
- c. Cascade algorithm
- d. Scaleogram

Guidance: level 1

:: Computational linguistics ::

The _____ is the international scientific and professional society for people working on problems involving natural language and computation. An annual meeting is held each summer in locations where significant computational linguistics research is carried out. It was founded in 1962, originally named the Association for Machine Translation and Computational Linguistics . It became the ACL in 1968.

Exam Probability: **Medium**

3. *Answer choices:*

(see index for correct answer)

- a. Distributional semantics
- b. Zeta distribution
- c. String grammar
- d. Association for Computational Linguistics

Guidance: level 1

:: Formal languages ::

In formal language theory, a _____ is a language generated by a context-free grammar .

Exam Probability: **Low**

4. *Answer choices:*

(see index for correct answer)

- a. Pumping lemma for context-free languages
- b. Categorial grammar
- c. Context-free language
- d. Simple precedence grammar

Guidance: level 1

:: Mathematical optimization ::

In evolutionary computation, _____ is a method that optimizes a problem by iteratively trying to improve a candidate solution with regard to a given measure of quality. Such methods are commonly known as metaheuristics as they make few or no assumptions about the problem being optimized and can search very large spaces of candidate solutions. However, metaheuristics such as DE do not guarantee an optimal solution is ever found.

Exam Probability: **Medium**

5. *Answer choices:*

(see index for correct answer)

- a. Semi-continuity
- b. Differential evolution
- c. Successive linear programming
- d. Vector optimization

Guidance: level 1

:: Artificial life ::

_____ is an artificial life software platform to study the evolutionary biology of self-replicating and evolving computer programs . _____ is under active development by Charles Ofria's Digital Evolution Lab at Michigan State University; the first version of _____ was designed in 1993 by Ofria, Chris Adami and C. Titus Brown at Caltech, and has been fully reengineered by Ofria on multiple occasions since then. The software was originally inspired by the Tierra system.

Exam Probability: **Low**

6. *Answer choices:*

(see index for correct answer)

- a. Astrochicken
- b. Grey goo
- c. Avida
- d. Santa Claus machine

Guidance: level 1

:: Computational science ::

The _____ , is a mathematical tool for reconstructing a volume-covering and continuous density or intensity field from a discrete point set. The DTFE has various astrophysical applications, such as the analysis of numerical simulations of cosmic structure formation, the mapping of the large-scale structure of the universe and improving computer simulation programs of cosmic structure formation. It has been developed by Willem Schaap and Rien van de Weijgaert. The main advantage of the DTFE is that it automatically adapts to variations in density and geometry. It is therefore very well suited for studies of the large scale galaxy distribution.

Exam Probability: **Medium**

7. *Answer choices:*

(see index for correct answer)

- a. Geometric design
- b. Lateral computing
- c. Computational electromagnetics
- d. Delaunay tessellation field estimator

Guidance: level 1

:: Numerical analysis ::

The word _____ is derived from Latin approximatus, from proximus meaning very near and the prefix ap- meaning to. Words like approximate, approximately and _____ are used especially in technical or scientific contexts. In everyday English, words such as roughly or around are used with a similar meaning. It is often found abbreviated as approx.

Exam Probability: **Low**

8. *Answer choices:*

(see index for correct answer)

- a. Pseudo-spectral method
- b. Significance arithmetic
- c. Approximation
- d. Discretization error

Guidance: level 1

:: Automata theory ::

In mathematics and theoretical computer science, an _____ is an infinite sequence of terms characterized by a finite automaton. The n-th term of an _____ a is a mapping of the final state reached in a finite automaton accepting the digits of the number n in some fixed base k.

Exam Probability: **High**

9. *Answer choices:*

(see index for correct answer)

- a. CIP-Tool
- b. Moore reduction procedure
- c. Timed automaton

- d. International Colloquium on Automata, Languages and Programming

Guidance: level 1

:: Formal languages ::

In computing, the _____ utility is a data comparison tool that calculates and displays the _____ erences between two files. Unlike edit distance notions used for other purposes, _____ is line-oriented rather than character-oriented, but it is like Levenshtein distance in that it tries to determine the smallest set of deletions and insertions to create one file from the other. The _____ command displays the changes made in a standard format, such that both humans and machines can understand the changes and apply them: given one file and the changes, the other file can be created.

Exam Probability: **High**

10. *Answer choices:*
(see index for correct answer)

- a. Left quotient
- b. Diff
- c. Intended interpretation
- d. Indexed language

Guidance: level 1

:: Computational science ::

_____ is a bioinformatics software company headquartered in Aarhus, Denmark, and with offices in Cambridge, Massachusetts, Tokyo, Taipei and Delhi. _____'s software has more than 250,000 users in more than 100 countries around the globe.

Exam Probability: **High**

11. *Answer choices:*

(see index for correct answer)

- a. Numerical analysis
- b. Autowave
- c. Tobias Preis
- d. CLC bio

Guidance: level 1

:: Computational complexity theory ::

A _____ is a representation for the computation steps of a non-deterministic Turing machine on a specified input. A _____ is a rooted tree of nodes and edges. Each node in the tree represents a single computational state, while each edge represents a transition to the next possible computation. The number of nodes of the tree is the size of the tree and the length of the path from the root to a given node is the depth of the node. The largest depth of an output node is the depth of the tree. The output nodes of the tree are called leaves.

Exam Probability: **Medium**

12. *Answer choices:*
(see index for correct answer)

- a. Pebble game
- b. Computation tree
- c. Randomness extractor
- d. Combinatorial search

Guidance: level 1

:: Computational science ::

_____ is a commercial application for DNA sequence assembly, sequence alignment, and editing on Mac OS X and Windows.

Exam Probability: **High**

13. *Answer choices:*

(see index for correct answer)

- a. CodonCode Aligner
- b. UGENE
- c. CLC bio
- d. Sidney Fernbach Award

Guidance: level 1

:: Dynamical systems ::

In mathematics and, in particular, mathematical dynamics, _____ and continuous time are two alternative frameworks within which to model variables that evolve over time.

Exam Probability: **Medium**

14. *Answer choices:*

(see index for correct answer)

- a. Irrational rotation
- b. Hamiltonian mechanics
- c. Wandering set
- d. Dynamical system

Guidance: level 1

:: Artificial intelligence ::

_____ is an inference method described colloquially as working backward from the goal. It is used in automated theorem provers, inference engines, proof assistants, and other artificial intelligence applications.

Exam Probability: **Medium**

15. *Answer choices:*

(see index for correct answer)

- a. Autonomic networking
- b. Zeuthen strategy
- c. Means-ends analysis
- d. Backward chaining

Guidance: level 1

:: Formal languages ::

In formal language theory, a _____ is a language that can be defined by a context-sensitive grammar. Context-sensitive is one of the four types of grammars in the Chomsky hierarchy.

Exam Probability: **High**

16. *Answer choices:*

(see index for correct answer)

- a. Indexed language
- b. Context-sensitive grammar
- c. Context-sensitive language
- d. Useless rules

Guidance: level 1

:: Artificial intelligence ::

_____ was a distributed computing project undertaken by Intelligence Realm, Inc. with the long-term goal of simulating the human brain in real time, complete with artificial consciousness and artificial general intelligence. They claimed to have found, in research, the "mechanisms of knowledge representation in the brain which is equivalent to finding artificial intelligence", before moving into the developmental phase.

Exam Probability: **High**

17. *Answer choices:*

(see index for correct answer)

- a. Artificial Intelligence System
- b. EasilyDo
- c. Recursive self improvement
- d. Attributional calculus

Guidance: level 1

:: Artificial life ::

An _____ is a collection of entities, each of which can be created catalytically by other entities within the set, such that as a whole, the set is able to catalyze its own production. In this way the set as a whole is said to be autocatalytic. _____ s were originally and most concretely defined in terms of molecular entities, but have more recently been metaphorically extended to the study of systems in sociology and economics.

Exam Probability: **Medium**

18. *Answer choices:*

(see index for correct answer)

- a. Avida
- b. Pacrat
- c. Evolving digital ecological networks
- d. Noble Ape

Guidance: level 1

:: Malware ::

A _____ is a standalone malware computer program that replicates itself in order to spread to other computers. Often, it uses a computer network to spread itself, relying on security failures on the target computer to access it. Worms almost always cause at least some harm to the network, even if only by consuming bandwidth, whereas viruses almost always corrupt or modify files on a targeted computer.

Exam Probability: **High**

19. *Answer choices:*

(see index for correct answer)

- a. Flame
- b. Crimeware
- c. Personal Internet Security 2011
- d. Computer worm

Guidance: level 1

:: Mathematical logic ::

_____ is an arrangement and organization of interrelated elements in a material object or system, or the object or system so organized. Material _____ s include man-made objects such as buildings and machines and natural objects such as biological organisms, minerals and chemicals. Abstract _____ s include data _____ s in computer science and musical form. Types of _____ include a hierarchy , a network featuring many-to-many links, or a lattice featuring connections between components that are neighbors in space.

Exam Probability: **Low**

20. *Answer choices:*

(see index for correct answer)

- a. Structure
- b. Metalogic
- c. Principia Mathematica
- d. Indicator function

Guidance: level 1

:: Formal sciences ::

_____ is an interdisciplinary field that develops methods and software tools for understanding biological data. As an interdisciplinary field of science, _____ combines biology, computer science, information engineering, mathematics and statistics to analyze and interpret biological data. _____ has been used for in silico analyses of biological queries using mathematical and statistical techniques.

Exam Probability: **Low**

21. *Answer choices:*

(see index for correct answer)

- a. Formal science
- b. Systems ecology

- c. Actuarial science
- d. Bioinformatics

Guidance: level 1

:: Computational complexity theory ::

In complexity theory, a time- _____ is a function f from natural numbers to natural numbers with the property that f can be constructed from n by a Turing machine in the time of order f. The purpose of such a definition is to exclude functions that do not provide an upper bound on the runtime of some Turing machine.

Exam Probability: **Medium**

22. *Answer choices:*
(see index for correct answer)

- a. Proof complexity
- b. Log-space reduction
- c. Constructible function
- d. Quantum complexity theory

Guidance: level 1

:: Theoretical computer science ::

_____ is one of the main ideas proposed by Stephen Wolfram in his book A New Kind of Science.

Exam Probability: **Low**

23. *Answer choices:*

(see index for correct answer)

- a. Computational irreducibility
- b. Idempotence
- c. pseudorandom
- d. Rough set

Guidance: level 1

:: Information theory ::

In information theory, the _____ is a result that relates to so-called "entropy power" of random variables. It shows that the entropy power of suitably well-behaved random variables is a superadditive function. The _____ was proved in 1948 by Claude Shannon in his seminal paper "A Mathematical Theory of Communication". Shannon also provided a sufficient condition for equality to hold; Stam showed that the condition is in fact necessary.

Exam Probability: **High**

24. *Answer choices:*

(see index for correct answer)

- a. Scale-free ideal gas
- b. Infonomics
- c. Entropy power inequality
- d. Pointwise mutual information

Guidance: level 1

:: Computational science ::

_____ is a broad field that attempts to optimize societal, economic, and environmental resources using methods from mathematics and computer science fields. Sustainability in this context is the ability to produce enough energy for the world to support its biological systems. Using the power of computers to process large quantities of information, decision making algorithms allocate resources based on real-time information.

Exam Probability: **Medium**

25. *Answer choices:*

(see index for correct answer)

- a. Autowave
- b. Computational Sustainability
- c. Newbler
- d. Atomistix Virtual NanoLab

Guidance: level 1

:: Mathematical optimization ::

In linear programming, _____, or opportunity cost, is the amount by which an objective function coefficient would have to improve before it would be possible for a corresponding variable to assume a positive value in the optimal solution. It is the cost for increasing a variable by a small amount, i.e., the first derivative from a certain point on the polyhedron that constrains the problem. When the point is a vertex in the polyhedron, the variable with the most extreme cost, negatively for minimization and positively maximization, is sometimes referred to as the steepest edge.

Exam Probability: **Medium**

26. *Answer choices:*

(see index for correct answer)

- a. Jeep problem
- b. Reduced cost
- c. Recursive economics
- d. Lagrange multipliers on Banach spaces

Guidance: level 1

:: Numerical analysis ::

In mathematics, a _____ is a numerical analysis technique used in computer simulation for solving ordinary differential equations by converting them to hyperbolic equations. In this way an explicit solution scheme is obtained with highly robust numerical properties. It was introduced by Auslander in 1968.

Exam Probability: **High**

27. *Answer choices:*

(see index for correct answer)

- a. Bi-directional delay line
- b. Approximation error
- c. Trigonometric tables
- d. Level set

Guidance: level 1

:: Computational complexity theory ::

In computational complexity theory, _____ is the usage of asymptotic analysis for the estimation of computational complexity of algorithms and computational problems, commonly associated with the usage of the big O notation.

Exam Probability: **Medium**

28. *Answer choices:*

(see index for correct answer)

- a. Configuration graph
- b. Communication complexity
- c. Electronic Colloquium on Computational Complexity
- d. Switching lemma

Guidance: level 1

:: Fourier analysis ::

The _____ decomposes a function of time into its constituent frequencies. This is similar to the way a musical chord can be expressed in terms of the volumes and frequencies of its constituent notes. The term _____ refers to both the frequency domain representation and the mathematical operation that associates the frequency domain representation to a function of time. The _____ of a function of time is itself a complex-valued function of frequency, whose magnitude component represents the amount of that frequency present in the original function, and whose complex argument is the phase offset of the basic sinusoid in that frequency. The _____ is not limited to functions of time, but the domain of the original function is commonly referred to as the time domain. There is also an inverse _____ that mathematically synthesizes the original function from its frequency domain representation.

Exam Probability: **Medium**

29. *Answer choices:*

(see index for correct answer)

- a. Marcinkiewicz interpolation theorem
- b. Modified discrete cosine transform
- c. Modulus of continuity
- d. Fourier transform

Guidance: level 1

:: Optimization algorithms and methods ::

In mathematical optimization, Dantzig's _____ is a popular algorithm for linear programming.

Exam Probability: **Medium**

30. *Answer choices:*
(see index for correct answer)

- a. Destination dispatch
- b. Rosenbrock methods
- c. Crew scheduling
- d. Simplex algorithm

Guidance: level 1

:: Formal languages ::

In computer science, an _____, or just syntax tree, is a tree representation of the abstract syntactic structure of source code written in a programming language. Each node of the tree denotes a construct occurring in the source code. The syntax is "abstract" in the sense that it does not represent every detail appearing in the real syntax, but rather just the structural, content-related details. For instance, grouping parentheses are implicit in the tree structure, and a syntactic construct like an if-condition-then expression may be denoted by means of a single node with three branches.

Exam Probability: **High**

31. *Answer choices:*

(see index for correct answer)

- a. Weak equivalence
- b. Concatenation
- c. Abstract syntax tree
- d. Descriptive interpretation

Guidance: level 1

:: Numerical analysis ::

_____ is the informal name of a mathematical reference work edited by Milton Abramowitz and Irene Stegun of the United States National Bureau of Standards, now the National Institute of Standards and Technology. Its full title is Handbook of Mathematical Functions with Formulas, Graphs, and Mathematical Tables. A digital successor to the Handbook was released as the "Digital Library of Mathematical Functions" on May 11, 2010, along with a printed version, the NIST Handbook of Mathematical Functions, published by Cambridge University Press.

Exam Probability: **Medium**

32. *Answer choices:*

(see index for correct answer)

- a. Finite-volume method
- b. Abramowitz and Stegun
- c. Truncation
- d. Numerical integration

Guidance: level 1

:: Spatial processes ::

In probability, statistics and related fields, a Poisson point process is a type of random mathematical object that consists of points randomly located on a mathematical space. The Poisson point process is often called simply the _____ , but it is also called a Poisson random measure, Poisson random point field or Poisson point field. This point process has convenient mathematical properties, which has led to it being frequently defined in Euclidean space and used as a mathematical model for seemingly random processes in numerous disciplines such as astronomy, biology, ecology, geology, seismology, physics, economics, image processing, and telecommunications.

Exam Probability: **Low**

33. *Answer choices:*

(see index for correct answer)

- a. Poisson process
- b. Boolean model
- c. Random field
- d. Superprocess

Guidance: level 1

:: Artificial life ::

The field bears some similarity to artificial life, but unlike artificial life, _____ focuses on the primary emergence of complex structures and processes of abiogenesis. _____ does not rely exclusively on the application of evolutionary computation and genetic algorithms to optimize artificial creatures or grow synthetic life forms. _____ instead studies systems of rules of interaction, initial conditions and primordial building blocks that can generate complex lifelike structures, based exclusively on repeated application of rules of interaction.

Exam Probability: **Medium**

34. *Answer choices:*

(see index for correct answer)

- a. Pacrat
- b. Astrochicken
- c. Creatures 3
- d. Artificial creation

Guidance: level 1

:: Databases ::

In information technology and computer science, especially in the fields of computer programming, operating systems, multiprocessors, and databases, _____ ensures that correct results for concurrent operations are generated, while getting those results as quickly as possible.

Exam Probability: **High**

35. *Answer choices:*

(see index for correct answer)

- a. Concurrency control
- b. Database virtualization
- c. DataEase
- d. World Integrated Trade Solution

Guidance: level 1

:: Formal methods ::

In theoretical computer science a _____ is a binary relation between state transition systems, associating systems that behave in the same way in the sense that one system simulates the other and vice versa.

Exam Probability: **Low**

36. *Answer choices:*

(see index for correct answer)

- a. Automated theorem proving
- b. Algebraic specification
- c. Bisimulation
- d. Liskov substitution principle

Guidance: level 1

:: Measurement ::

In statistics, a _____ is a type of interval estimate, computed from the statistics of the observed data, that might contain the true value of an unknown population parameter. The interval has an associated confidence level that, loosely speaking, quantifies the level of confidence that the parameter lies in the interval. More strictly speaking, the confidence level represents the frequency of possible _____ s that contain the true value of the unknown population parameter. In other words, if _____ s are constructed using a given confidence level from an infinite number of independent sample statistics, the proportion of those intervals that contain the true value of the parameter will be equal to the confidence level.

Exam Probability: **Medium**

37. *Answer choices:*

(see index for correct answer)

- a. Random error
- b. Confidence interval
- c. Physical constant
- d. WELMEC

Guidance: level 1

:: Fourier analysis ::

In mathematics, the _____ is an integral transform named after its inventor Pierre-Simon Laplace. It takes a function of a real variable t to a function of a complex variable s. The transform has many applications in science and engineering.

Exam Probability: **Low**

38. *Answer choices:*

(see index for correct answer)

- a. S plane
- b. Metaplectic group
- c. Solid harmonics
- d. Spectral concentration problem

Guidance: level 1

:: Numerical analysis ::

In numerical analysis, computational physics, and simulation, _____ is the error resulting from the fact that a function of a continuous variable is represented in the computer by a finite number of evaluations, for example, on a lattice. _____ can usually be reduced by using a more finely spaced lattice, with an increased computational cost.

Exam Probability: **Low**

39. *Answer choices:*

(see index for correct answer)

- a. Levinson recursion
- b. Kahan summation algorithm
- c. Interval propagation
- d. Successive parabolic interpolation

Guidance: level 1

:: Formal methods ::

_____ is the linguistic and philosophical study of meaning, in language, programming languages, formal logics, and semiotics. It is concerned with the relationship between signifiers—like words, phrases, signs, and symbols—and what they stand for in reality, their denotation.

Exam Probability: **Low**

40. *Answer choices:*

(see index for correct answer)

- a. Model-based specification
- b. Concurrency semantics
- c. Production equipment control
- d. Applicative Universal Grammar

Guidance: level 1

:: Formal languages ::

In computer text processing, a _____ is a system for annotating a document in a way that is syntactically distinguishable from the text. The idea and terminology evolved from the "marking up" of paper manuscripts, i.e., the revision instructions by editors, traditionally written with a red or blue pencil on authors' manuscripts. In digital media this "blue pencil instruction text" was replaced by tags, which indicate what the parts of the document are, rather than details of how they might be shown on some display. This lets authors avoid formatting every instance of the same kind of thing redundantly. It also avoids the specification of fonts and dimensions, which may not apply to many users.

Exam Probability: **Low**

41. *Answer choices:*
(see index for correct answer)

- a. Greibach normal form
- b. L-system
- c. Erasing rule
- d. Kuroda normal form

Guidance: level 1

:: Programming language topics ::

In formal language theory, a _____ is a certain type of formal grammar: a set of production rules that describe all possible strings in a given formal language. Production rules are simple replacements. For example, the rule

Exam Probability: **Medium**

42. *Answer choices:*

(see index for correct answer)

- a. Parametricity
- b. Program optimization
- c. Abstraction principle
- d. Context-free grammar

Guidance: level 1

:: Theory of computation ::

In computability theory a _____ is a special kind of numbering first introduced by Yuri L. Ershov in 1973.

Exam Probability: **Low**

43. *Answer choices:*

(see index for correct answer)

- a. Computable function
- b. Admissible numbering
- c. Cylindric numbering
- d. Description number

Guidance: level 1

:: Theory of computation ::

In computability theory, the _____ is the problem of determining, from a description of an arbitrary computer program and an input, whether the program will finish running or continue to run forever.

Exam Probability: **Medium**

44. *Answer choices:*
(see index for correct answer)

- a. Halting problem
- b. Scale factor
- c. Primitive recursive function
- d. Parallel computation thesis

Guidance: level 1

:: Queueing theory ::

In probability theory, the _____ , Lindley recursion or Lindley processes is a discrete-time stochastic process An where n takes integer values and.

Exam Probability: **Medium**

45. *Answer choices:*

(see index for correct answer)

- a. Lindley equation
- b. Teletraffic engineering
- c. Palm calculus
- d. Jackson network

Guidance: level 1

:: Computational science ::

_____ , computational electrodynamics or electromagnetic modeling is the process of modeling the interaction of electromagnetic fields with physical objects and the environment.

Exam Probability: **Medium**

46. *Answer choices:*

(see index for correct answer)

- a. Plane wave expansion method
- b. Phyloscan
- c. Computational electromagnetics
- d. Projector augmented wave method

Guidance: level 1

:: Artificial life ::

An _____ is a chemical-like system that usually consists of objects, called molecules, that interact according to rules resembling chemical reaction rules. Artificial chemistries are created and studied in order to understand fundamental properties of chemical systems, including prebiotic evolution, as well as for developing chemical computing systems. _____ is a field within computer science wherein chemical reactions—often biochemical ones—are computer-simulated, yielding insights on evolution, self-assembly, and other biochemical phenomena. The field does not use actual chemicals, and should not be confused with either synthetic chemistry or computational chemistry. Rather, bits of information are used to represent the starting molecules, and the end products are examined along with the processes that led to them. The field originated in artificial life but has shown to be a versatile method with applications in many fields such as chemistry, economics, sociology and linguistics.

Exam Probability: **Medium**

47. *Answer choices:*

(see index for correct answer)

- a. Avida

- b. Artificial creation
- c. Sniffy: The Virtual Rat
- d. Artificial chemistry

Guidance: level 1

:: Computational science ::

The _____ is a method for computing scattering of radiation by particles of arbitrary shape and by periodic structures. Given a target of arbitrary geometry, one seeks to calculate its scattering and absorption properties. Exact solutions to Maxwell's equations are known only for special geometries such as spheres, spheroids, or cylinders, so approximate methods are in general required. However, the DDA employs no physical approximations and can produce accurate enough results, given sufficient computer power.

Exam Probability: **Medium**

48. *Answer choices:*
(see index for correct answer)

- a. European Conference on Computational Biology
- b. Enthought
- c. Projector augmented wave method
- d. Discrete dipole approximation

Guidance: level 1

:: Computational complexity theory ::

In computational complexity theory, a _____ is a set of problems of related resource-based complexity. A typical _____ has a definition of the form.

Exam Probability: **Low**

49. *Answer choices:*
(see index for correct answer)

- a. Combinatorial search
- b. The Complexity of Songs
- c. Complexity class
- d. Existential theory of the reals

Guidance: level 1

:: Theory of computation ::

The _____ is a theoretical model of computation introduced by Samuel Eilenberg in 1974. The X in " _____ " represents the fundamental data type on which the machine operates; for example, a machine that operates on databases would be a database-machine. The _____ model is structurally the same as the finite state machine, except that the symbols used to label the machine's transitions denote relations of type XX. Crossing a transition is equivalent to applying the relation that labels it, and traversing a path in the machine corresponds to applying all the associated relations, one after the other.

Exam Probability: **High**

50. *Answer choices:*

(see index for correct answer)

- a. Computable function
- b. Ten15
- c. X-Machine
- d. Post correspondence problem

Guidance: level 1

:: Theoretical computer science conferences ::

The _____ is the premier academic _____ and related fields. The first CADE was organized in 1974 at the Argonne National Laboratory near Chicago. Most CADE meetings have been held in Europe and the United States. However, conferences have been held all over the world. Since 1996, CADE has been held yearly. In 2001, CADE was, for the first time, merged into the International Joint Conference on Automated Reasoning . This has been repeated biannually since 2004.

Exam Probability: **High**

51. *Answer choices:*

(see index for correct answer)

- a. International Conference on Automated Reasoning with Analytic Tableaux and Related Methods
- b. International Symposium on Distributed Computing
- c. Conference on Automated Deduction
- d. Symposium on Parallelism in Algorithms and Architectures

Guidance: level 1

:: Theoretical computer science ::

In computer science, _____ is a type of operation that is dual to recursion. Whereas recursion works analytically, starting on data further from a base case and breaking it down into smaller data and repeating until one reaches a base case, _____ works synthetically, starting from a base case and building it up, iteratively producing data further removed from a base case. Put simply, corecursive algorithms use the data that they themselves produce, bit by bit, as they become available, and needed, to produce further bits of data. A similar but distinct concept is generative recursion which may lack a definite "direction" inherent in _____ and recursion.

Exam Probability: **Low**

52. *Answer choices:*

(see index for correct answer)

- a. Probabilistic bisimulation
- b. Computational problem
- c. Corecursion
- d. Neighbour-sensing model

Guidance: level 1

:: Monte Carlo methods ::

In statistics, _____ is a general technique for estimating properties of a particular distribution, while only having samples generated from a different distribution than the distribution of interest. It is related to umbrella sampling in computational physics. Depending on the application, the term may refer to the process of sampling from this alternative distribution, the process of inference, or both.

Exam Probability: **Medium**

53. *Answer choices:*

(see index for correct answer)

- a. Monte Carlo localization
- b. Monte Carlo integration
- c. Importance sampling
- d. Tau-leaping

Guidance: level 1

:: Mathematical optimization ::

_____ is a branch of multiobjective optimization, which in turn is a branch of multi-criteria decision analysis. This is an optimization programme. It can be thought of as an extension or generalisation of linear programming to handle multiple, normally conflicting objective measures. Each of these measures is given a goal or target value to be achieved. Unwanted deviations from this set of target values are then minimised in an achievement function. This can be a vector or a weighted sum dependent on the _____ variant used. As satisfaction of the target is deemed to satisfy the decision maker, an underlying satisficing philosophy is assumed. _____ is used to perform three types of analysis.

Exam Probability: **High**

54. *Answer choices:*

(see index for correct answer)

- a. Optimal design
- b. Goal programming
- c. Trajectory optimization
- d. Extended newsvendor model

Guidance: level 1

:: Theoretical computer science ::

_____ is a branch of computing which uses DNA, biochemistry, and molecular biology hardware, instead of the traditional silicon-based computer technologies. Research and development in this area concerns theory, experiments, and applications of _____ . The term "molectronics" has sometimes been used, but this term has already been used for an earlier technology, a then-unsuccessful rival of the first integrated circuits; this term has also been used more generally, for molecular-scale electronic technology.

Exam Probability: **Medium**

55. *Answer choices:*

(see index for correct answer)

- a. DNA computing
- b. Complexity function
- c. European Association for Theoretical Computer Science
- d. Scientific community metaphor

Guidance: level 1

:: Theory of computation ::

Informally, in theoretical computer science, the _____ game aims at finding a terminating program of a given size that produces the most output possible.

Exam Probability: **Low**

56. Answer choices:

(see index for correct answer)

- a. Blockhead
- b. Hypercomputation
- c. Nomogram
- d. Post correspondence problem

Guidance: level 1

:: Computer arithmetic algorithms ::

In computer science, _____ , also called bignum arithmetic, multiple-precision arithmetic, or sometimes infinite-precision arithmetic, indicates that calculations are performed on numbers whose digits of precision are limited only by the available memory of the host system. This contrasts with the faster fixed-precision arithmetic found in most arithmetic logic unit hardware, which typically offers between 8 and 64 bits of precision.

Exam Probability: **High**

57. Answer choices:

(see index for correct answer)

- a. AGM method
- b. Division algorithm
- c. Spigot algorithm
- d. Karatsuba algorithm

Guidance: level 1

:: Mathematical optimization ::

In artificial intelligence, _____ is a technique of evolving programs, starting from a population of unfit programs, fit for a particular task by applying operations analogous to natural genetic processes to the population of programs. It is essentially a heuristic search technique often described as 'hill climbing', i.e. searching for an optimal or at least suitable program among the space of all programs.

Exam Probability: **Medium**

58. *Answer choices:*
(see index for correct answer)

- a. Extended newsvendor model
- b. Topological derivative
- c. Duality gap
- d. Genetic programming

Guidance: level 1

:: Formal languages ::

In computer science, an _____ is a context-free grammar for which there exists a string that can have more than one leftmost derivation or parse tree, while an un _____ is a context-free grammar for which every valid string has a unique leftmost derivation or parse tree. Many languages admit both ambiguous and un _____ s, while some languages admit only _____ s. Any non-empty language admits an _____ by taking an un _____ and introducing a duplicate rule or synonym. A language that only admits _____ s is called an inherently ambiguous language, and there are inherently ambiguous context-free languages. Deterministic context-free grammars are always unambiguous, and are an important subclass of un _____ s; there are non-deterministic un _____ s, however.

Exam Probability: **Medium**

59. *Answer choices:*

(see index for correct answer)

- a. Unrestricted grammar
- b. Montague grammar
- c. Empty string
- d. Ambiguous grammar

Guidance: level 1

Information technology

Information technology is the use of computers to store, retrieve, transmit, and manipulate data, or information, often in the context of a business or other enterprise. IT is considered to be a subset of information and communications technology.

:: Data security ::

In financial accounting, an _____ is any resource owned by the business. Anything tangible or intangible that can be owned or controlled to produce value and that is held by a company to produce positive economic value is an _____ . Simply stated, _____ s represent value of ownership that can be converted into cash . The balance sheet of a firm records the monetary value of the _____ s owned by that firm. It covers money and other valuables belonging to an individual or to a business.

Exam Probability: **Medium**

1. *Answer choices:*

(see index for correct answer)

- a. Asset
- b. Air gap
- c. Data theft
- d. Extrusion detection

Guidance: level 1

:: Information science ::

_____ is the resolution of uncertainty; it is that which answers the question of "what an entity is" and thus defines both its essence and nature of its characteristics. _____ relates to both data and knowledge, as data is meaningful _____ representing values attributed to parameters, and knowledge signifies understanding of a concept. _____ is uncoupled from an observer, which is an entity that can access _____ and thus discern what it specifies; _____ exists beyond an event horizon for example. In the case of knowledge, the _____ itself requires a cognitive observer to be obtained.

Exam Probability: **Low**

2. *Answer choices:*

(see index for correct answer)

- a. Information
- b. Mathematical knowledge management
- c. Education informatics
- d. Media ecology

Guidance: level 1

:: Malware ::

_____ is any software intentionally designed to cause damage to a computer, server, client, or computer network. _____ does the damage after it is implanted or introduced in some way into a target's computer and can take the form of executable code, scripts, active content, and other software. The code is described as computer viruses, worms, Trojan horses, ransomware, spyware, adware, and scareware, among other terms. _____ has a malicious intent, acting against the interest of the computer user—and so does not include software that causes unintentional harm due to some deficiency, which is typically described as a software bug.

Exam Probability: **Medium**

3. *Answer choices:*

(see index for correct answer)

- a. 3wPlayer
- b. Clickjacking
- c. Man-in-the-browser
- d. Malware

Guidance: level 1

:: Control characters ::

_____ is the boundless three-dimensional extent in which objects and events have relative position and direction. Physical _____ is often conceived in three linear dimensions, although modern physicists usually consider it, with time, to be part of a boundless four-dimensional continuum known as _____ time. The concept of _____ is considered to be of fundamental importance to an understanding of the physical universe. However, disagreement continues between philosophers over whether it is itself an entity, a relationship between entities, or part of a conceptual framework.

Exam Probability: **Medium**

4. *Answer choices:*

(see index for correct answer)

- a. Zero-width joiner
- b. Block check character
- c. Carriage return
- d. Space

Guidance: level 1

:: Computer networking ::

_____ is the concept of businesses electronically communicating information that was traditionally communicated on paper, such as purchase orders and invoices. Technical standards for EDI exist to facilitate parties transacting such instruments without having to make special arrangements.

Exam Probability: **Low**

5. *Answer choices:*

(see index for correct answer)

- a. Electronic data interchange
- b. Global network
- c. Cablefree
- d. In situ adaptive tabulation

Guidance: level 1

:: Data types ::

_____ is a relation between objects in which one object designates, or acts as a means by which to connect to or link to, another object. The first object in this relation is said to refer to the second object. It is called a name for the second object. The second object, the one to which the first object refers, is called the referent of the first object. A name is usually a phrase or expression, or some other symbolic representation. Its referent may be anything – a material object, a person, an event, an activity, or an abstract concept.

Exam Probability: **Low**

6. *Answer choices:*

(see index for correct answer)

- a. Real data type
- b. Reference
- c. Set
- d. Object

Guidance: level 1

:: Malware ::

The _____ is a story from the Trojan War about the subterfuge that the Greeks used to enter the independent city of Troy and win the war. In the canonical version, after a fruitless 10-year siege, the Greeks constructed a huge wooden horse, and hid a select force of men inside including Odysseus. The Greeks pretended to sail away, and the Trojans pulled the horse into their city as a victory trophy. That night the Greek force crept out of the horse and opened the gates for the rest of the Greek army, which had sailed back under cover of night. The Greeks entered and destroyed the city of Troy, ending the war.

Exam Probability: **Low**

7. *Answer choices:*

(see index for correct answer)

- a. Trojan horse
- b. Malvertisement
- c. PUM.bad.proxy
- d. Mobile code

Guidance: level 1

:: Cloud applications ::

_____ is a software licensing and delivery model in which software is licensed on a subscription basis and is centrally hosted. It is sometimes referred to as "on-demand software", and was formerly referred to as "software plus services" by Microsoft. SaaS is typically accessed by users using a thin client, e.g. via a web browser. SaaS has become a common delivery model for many business applications, including office software, messaging software, payroll processing software, DBMS software, management software, CAD software, development software, gamification, virtualization, accounting, collaboration, customer relationship management , Management Information Systems , enterprise resource planning , invoicing, human resource management , talent acquisition, learning management systems, content management , Geographic Information Systems , and service desk management. SaaS has been incorporated into the strategy of nearly all leading enterprise software companies.

Exam Probability: **High**

8. *Answer choices:*

(see index for correct answer)

- a. My Phone
- b. QuestionPro.com
- c. Google Cloud Connect
- d. Janrain

Guidance: level 1

:: Data management ::

_____ comprises the strategies and technologies used by enterprises for the data analysis of business information. BI technologies provide historical, current and predictive views of business operations. Common functions of _____ technologies include reporting, online analytical processing, analytics, data mining, process mining, complex event processing, business performance management, benchmarking, text mining, predictive analytics and prescriptive analytics. BI technologies can handle large amounts of structured and sometimes unstructured data to help identify, develop and otherwise create new strategic business opportunities. They aim to allow for the easy interpretation of these big data. Identifying new opportunities and implementing an effective strategy based on insights can provide businesses with a competitive market advantage and long-term stability.

Exam Probability: **Medium**

9. *Answer choices:*

(see index for correct answer)

- a. Data architecture
- b. Data deduplication
- c. Business intelligence
- d. ROOT

Guidance: level 1

:: Data processing ::

_____ is, generally, "the collection and manipulation of items of data to produce meaningful information." In this sense it can be considered a subset of information processing, "the change of information in any manner detectable by an observer."

Exam Probability: **Low**

10. *Answer choices:*

(see index for correct answer)

- a. Data processing technician
- b. Association of Information Technology Professionals
- c. Information technology audit
- d. Data processing

Guidance: level 1

:: Computing output devices ::

An _____ is any piece of computer hardware equipment which converts information into human-readable form.

Exam Probability: **Medium**

11. *Answer choices:*

(see index for correct answer)

- a. MyVu
- b. DR37-P
- c. Output device
- d. Palette

Guidance: level 1

:: Reasoning ::

In logic and philosophy, an _____ is a series of statements, called the premises or premisses, intended to determine the degree of truth of another statement, the conclusion. The logical form of an _____ in a natural language can be represented in a symbolic formal language, and independently of natural language formally defined " _____ s" can be made in math and computer science.

Exam Probability: **Medium**

12. *Answer choices:*
(see index for correct answer)

- a. Irrationality
- b. Practical reason
- c. Argument
- d. Principle of sufficient reason

Guidance: level 1

:: Software ::

Computer _____ , or simply _____ , is a collection of data or computer instructions that tell the computer how to work. This is in contrast to physical hardware, from which the system is built and actually performs the work. In computer science and _____ engineering, computer _____ is all information processed by computer systems, programs and data. Computer _____ includes computer programs, libraries and related non-executable data, such as online documentation or digital media. Computer hardware and _____ require each other and neither can be realistically used on its own.

Exam Probability: **High**

13. *Answer choices:*

(see index for correct answer)

- a. EZ-Frame
- b. Name generator
- c. Bibledit
- d. Software

Guidance: level 1

:: Game theory ::

To _____ is to make a deal between different parties where each party gives up part of their demand. In arguments, _____ is a concept of finding agreement through communication, through a mutual acceptance of terms—often involving variations from an original goal or desires.

Exam Probability: **Medium**

14. *Answer choices:*

(see index for correct answer)

- a. Competitive altruism
- b. Michael Taylor
- c. Wait/walk dilemma
- d. Compromise

Guidance: level 1

:: Operations research ::

_____ refers to a business or organization attempting to acquire goods or services to accomplish its goals. Although there are several organizations that attempt to set standards in the _____ process, processes can vary greatly between organizations. Typically the word "_____" is not used interchangeably with the word "procurement", since procurement typically includes expediting, supplier quality, and transportation and logistics in addition to _____ .

Exam Probability: **Medium**

15. Answer choices:

(see index for correct answer)

- a. Economic production quantity
- b. Flow network
- c. Industrial engineering
- d. Purchasing

Guidance: level 1

:: Utility ::

Within economics the concept of _____ is used to model worth or value, but its usage has evolved significantly over time. The term was introduced initially as a measure of pleasure or satisfaction within the theory of utilitarianism by moral philosophers such as Jeremy Bentham and John Stuart Mill. But the term has been adapted and reapplied within neoclassical economics, which dominates modern economic theory, as a _____ function that represents a consumer's preference ordering over a choice set. As such, it is devoid of its original interpretation as a measurement of the pleasure or satisfaction obtained by the consumer from that choice.

Exam Probability: **Medium**

16. Answer choices:

(see index for correct answer)

- a. Indirect utility function
- b. Rank-dependent expected utility

- c. Utility
- d. Marginal utility

Guidance: level 1

:: Virtual economy ::

_____ is an online virtual world, developed and owned by the San Francisco-based firm Linden Lab and launched on June 23, 2003. By 2013, _____ had approximately one million regular users; at the end of 2017 active user count totals "between 800,000 and 900,000". In many ways, _____ is similar to massively multiplayer online role-playing games; however, Linden Lab is emphatic that their creation is not a game: "There is no manufactured conflict, no set objective".

Exam Probability: **Medium**

17. *Answer choices:*
(see index for correct answer)

- a. Fairyland
- b. Gold farming in China
- c. Space flight simulator game
- d. Second Life

Guidance: level 1

:: Photo software ::

_____ was an augmented reality translation application from Quest Visual. _____ used the built-in cameras on smartphones and similar devices to quickly scan and identify foreign text , and then translate and display the words in another language on the device's display. The words were displayed in the original context on the original background, and the translation was performed in real-time without connection to the internet. For example, using the viewfinder of a camera to show a shop sign on a smartphone's display would result in a real-time image of the shop sign being displayed, but the words shown on the sign would be the translated words instead of the original foreign words.

Exam Probability: **High**

18. *Answer choices:*

(see index for correct answer)

- a. Helicon Focus
- b. Dynamic Photo HDR
- c. Adobe Photoshop Lightroom
- d. PhotoScape

Guidance: level 1

:: Software design ::

_____ is the process of defining the architecture, modules, interfaces, and data for a system to satisfy specified requirements. _____ could be seen as the application of systems theory to product development. There is some overlap with the disciplines of systems analysis, systems architecture and systems engineering.

Exam Probability: **Low**

19. *Answer choices:*

(see index for correct answer)

- a. Design process
- b. Software design
- c. Systems design
- d. Interactive design

Guidance: level 1

:: World Wide Web Consortium standards ::

Hypertext Markup Language is the standard markup language for creating web pages and web applications. With Cascading Style Sheets and JavaScript, it forms a triad of cornerstone technologies for the World Wide Web.

Exam Probability: **Medium**

20. *Answer choices:*

(see index for correct answer)

- a. HTML5
- b. Document Object Model
- c. Html
- d. Polyglot markup

Guidance: level 1

:: Artificial intelligence ::

In computer science, _____, sometimes called machine intelligence, is intelligence demonstrated by machines, in contrast to the natural intelligence displayed by humans and animals. Colloquially, the term "_____" is used to describe machines that mimic "cognitive" functions that humans associate with other human minds, such as "learning" and "problem solving".

Exam Probability: **Low**

21. *Answer choices:*

(see index for correct answer)

- a. Any-angle path planning
- b. Maluuba
- c. ACROSS Project
- d. AgentSheets

Guidance: level 1

:: Database management systems ::

_____ s or data _____ s are computer languages used to make queries in databases and information systems.

Exam Probability: **Medium**

22. *Answer choices:*

(see index for correct answer)

- a. Query language
- b. Data control language
- c. Object Exchange Model
- d. Cursor

Guidance: level 1

:: E-commerce ::

_____ is the activity of buying or selling of products on online services or over the Internet. Electronic commerce draws on technologies such as mobile commerce, electronic funds transfer, supply chain management, Internet marketing, online transaction processing, electronic data interchange, inventory management systems, and automated data collection systems.

Exam Probability: **High**

23. *Answer choices:*

(see index for correct answer)

- a. Shipping portal
- b. Click Frenzy
- c. Diversify BPO
- d. E-commerce

Guidance: level 1

:: Graphical user interface elements ::

A _____ is an opening in a wall, door, roof or vehicle that allows the passage of light, sound, and air. Modern _____ s are usually glazed or covered in some other transparent or translucent material, a sash set in a frame in the opening; the sash and frame are also referred to as a _____ . Many glazed _____ s may be opened, to allow ventilation, or closed, to exclude inclement weather. _____ s often have a latch or similar mechanism to lock the _____ shut or to hold it open by various amounts.

Exam Probability: **High**

24. *Answer choices:*

(see index for correct answer)

- a. Dialog box
- b. modal dialog
- c. Address bar
- d. Window

Guidance: level 1

:: Virtual reality ::

_____ is an experience taking place within simulated and immersive environments that can be similar to or completely different from the real world. Applications of _____ can include entertainment and educational purposes. Other, distinct types of VR style technology include augmented reality and mixed reality.

Exam Probability: **Low**

25. *Answer choices:*

(see index for correct answer)

- a. Virtual reality
- b. Avizo

- c. ST1080
- d. Virtual engineering

Guidance: level 1

:: Computer file systems ::

In computing, a _____ or filesystem controls how data is stored and retrieved. Without a _____ , information placed in a storage medium would be one large body of data with no way to tell where one piece of information stops and the next begins. By separating the data into pieces and giving each piece a name, the information is easily isolated and identified. Taking its name from the way paper-based information systems are named, each group of data is called a "file". The structure and logic rules used to manage the groups of information and their names is called a "_____".

Exam Probability: **Low**

26. *Answer choices:*

(see index for correct answer)

- a. File system
- b. Archive file
- c. Directory
- d. Crash counting

Guidance: level 1

:: Decision theory ::

An _____, also known as an <u>Executive support system</u>, is a type of management support system that facilitates and supports senior executive information and decision-making needs. It provides easy access to internal and external information relevant to organizational goals. It is commonly considered a specialized form of decision support system.

Exam Probability: **High**

27. *Answer choices:*

(see index for correct answer)

- a. Causal decision theory
- b. Seven Management and Planning Tools
- c. Consensus-seeking decision-making
- d. Simple prioritization

Guidance: level 1

:: Integrated development environments ::

_____ is a third-generation event-driven programming language from Microsoft for its Component Object Model programming model first released in 1991 and declared legacy during 2008. Microsoft intended _____ to be relatively easy to learn and use. _____ was derived from BASIC and enables the rapid application development of graphical user interface applications, access to databases using Data Access Objects, Remote Data Objects, or ActiveX Data Objects, and creation of ActiveX controls and objects.

Exam Probability: **High**

28. *Answer choices:*

(see index for correct answer)

- a. DrJava
- b. Softune
- c. ANTLR Studio
- d. Service Development Studio

Guidance: level 1

:: Holism ::

_____ characterises the behaviour of a system or model whose components interact in multiple ways and follow local rules, meaning there is no reasonable higher instruction to define the various possible interactions.

Exam Probability: **Medium**

29. *Answer choices:*

(see index for correct answer)

- a. Structured programming
- b. Law of Complexity/Consciousness
- c. Holarchy
- d. Complexity

Guidance: level 1

:: Data centers ::

A _____ or data centre is a building, dedicated space within a building, or a group of buildings used to house computer systems and associated components, such as telecommunications and storage systems.

Exam Probability: **Low**

30. *Answer choices:*

(see index for correct answer)

- a. Data center
- b. Energy Logic
- c. Swiss Fort Knox
- d. CyberBunker

Guidance: level 1

:: Decision theory ::

A _____ is an information system used for decision-making, and for the coordination, control, analysis, and visualization of information in an organization; especially in a company.

Exam Probability: **High**

31. *Answer choices:*

(see index for correct answer)

- a. Recognition primed decision
- b. Management information system
- c. Analytic network process
- d. Spatial decision support system

Guidance: level 1

:: Mereology ::

_____ , in the abstract, is what belongs to or with something, whether as an attribute or as a component of said thing. In the context of this article, it is one or more components , whether physical or incorporeal, of a person's estate; or so belonging to, as in being owned by, a person or jointly a group of people or a legal entity like a corporation or even a society. Depending on the nature of the _____ , an owner of _____ has the right to consume, alter, share, redefine, rent, mortgage, pawn, sell, exchange, transfer, give away or destroy it, or to exclude others from doing these things, as well as to perhaps abandon it; whereas regardless of the nature of the _____ , the owner thereof has the right to properly use it , or at the very least exclusively keep it.

Exam Probability: **Low**

32. *Answer choices:*

(see index for correct answer)

- a. Property
- b. Non-wellfounded mereology
- c. Mereological essentialism
- d. Meronomy

Guidance: level 1

:: Educational programming languages ::

A _____ is a physiological capacity of organisms that provides data for perception. The _____ s and their operation, classification, and theory are overlapping topics studied by a variety of fields, most notably neuroscience, cognitive psychology, and philosophy of perception. The nervous system has a specific sensory nervous system, and a _____ organ, or sensor, dedicated to each _____ .

Exam Probability: **Low**

33. *Answer choices:*

(see index for correct answer)

- a. UCBLogo
- b. PL/C
- c. Gofer
- d. ECL programming language

Guidance: level 1

:: Business software ::

The _____ is a strategy performance management tool – a semi-standard structured report, that can be used by managers to keep track of the execution of activities by the staff within their control and to monitor the consequences arising from these actions.

Exam Probability: **Low**

34. *Answer choices:*

(see index for correct answer)

- a. USAS
- b. Business Control Layer
- c. Replicon
- d. Hyperion Planning

Guidance: level 1

:: Information appliances ::

_____ is a line of smartphones, tablets, and services originally designed and marketed by Canadian company _____ Limited. These are currently designed, manufactured, and marketed by TCL Communication, BB Merah Putih, and Optiemus Infracom for the global, Indonesian, and South Asian markets using the _____ brand under license.

Exam Probability: **Low**

35. *Answer choices:*

(see index for correct answer)

- a. Information appliance
- b. BlackBerry
- c. Mobile device
- d. Internet tablet

Guidance: level 1

:: Management ::

_____ is the practice of initiating, planning, executing, controlling, and closing the work of a team to achieve specific goals and meet specific success criteria at the specified time.

Exam Probability: **High**

36. *Answer choices:*

(see index for correct answer)

- a. performance measurement
- b. Continuous monitoring
- c. Project management
- d. Innovation management

Guidance: level 1

:: Transaction processing ::

Transaction processing is a way of computing that divides work into individual, indivisible operations, called transactions. A _____ is a software system, or software/hardware combination, that supports transaction processing.

Exam Probability: **Medium**

37. *Answer choices:*

(see index for correct answer)

- a. Transaction processing system
- b. Transactional memory
- c. Multiversion concurrency control
- d. Purchase-to-pay

Guidance: level 1

:: Customer relationship management software ::

Customer-relationship management is an approach to manage a company's interaction with current and potential customers. It uses data analysis about customers' history with a company to improve business relationships with customers, specifically focusing on customer retention and ultimately driving sales growth.

Exam Probability: **Low**

38. *Answer choices:*

(see index for correct answer)

- a. InContact
- b. Serial switcher
- c. Access Commerce
- d. Customer relationship management

Guidance: level 1

:: Causal inference ::

An _____ is a procedure carried out to support, refute, or validate a hypothesis. _____ s provide insight into cause-and-effect by demonstrating what outcome occurs when a particular factor is manipulated. _____ s vary greatly in goal and scale, but always rely on repeatable procedure and logical analysis of the results. There also exists natural _____ al studies.

Exam Probability: **Low**

39. *Answer choices:*

(see index for correct answer)

- a. Experiment
- b. External validity
- c. Inductive reasoning
- d. Principal stratification

Guidance: level 1

:: Cloud clients ::

_____ is a line of smartphones designed and marketed by Apple Inc. All generations of the _____ use Apple's iOS mobile operating system software. The first-generation _____ was released on June 29, 2007, and multiple new hardware iterations with new iOS releases have been released since.

Exam Probability: **Low**

40. *Answer choices:*

(see index for correct answer)

- a. IPhone
- b. OG-OS
- c. OPhone
- d. Chromebook

Guidance: level 1

:: Evaluation methods ::

_____ is asystematic determination of a subject's merit, worth and significance, using criteria governed by a set of standards. It can assist an organization, program, design, project or any other intervention or initiative to assess any aim, realisable concept/proposal, or any alternative, to help in decision-making; or to ascertain the degree of achievement or value in regard to the aim and objectives and results of any such action that has been completed. The primary purpose of _____, in addition to gaining insight into prior or existing initiatives, is to enable reflection and assist in the identification of future change.

Exam Probability: **Low**

41. *Answer choices:*

(see index for correct answer)

- a. Quality audit
- b. Evaluation
- c. Adaptive comparative judgement
- d. Terahertz nondestructive evaluation

Guidance: level 1

:: Supply chain management terms ::

In business and finance, _____ is a system of organizations, people, activities, information, and resources involved in moving a product or service from supplier to customer. _____ activities involve the transformation of natural resources, raw materials, and components into a finished product that is delivered to the end customer. In sophisticated _____ systems, used products may re-enter the _____ at any point where residual value is recyclable. _____ s link value chains.

Exam Probability: **Low**

42. *Answer choices:*

(see index for correct answer)

- a. Supply chain management
- b. Supply chain

Guidance: level 1

:: Mathematical logic ::

_____ is an arrangement and organization of interrelated elements in a material object or system, or the object or system so organized. Material _____ s include man-made objects such as buildings and machines and natural objects such as biological organisms, minerals and chemicals. Abstract _____ s include data _____ s in computer science and musical form. Types of _____ include a hierarchy, a network featuring many-to-many links, or a lattice featuring connections between components that are neighbors in space.

Exam Probability: **Low**

43. *Answer choices:*

(see index for correct answer)

- a. Principia Mathematica
- b. Structure
- c. Formal calculation
- d. Predicate

Guidance: level 1

:: Computer network security ::

_____ is software that aims to gather information about a person or organization, sometimes without their knowledge, that may send such information to another entity without the consumer's consent, that asserts control over a device without the consumer's knowledge, or it may send such information to another entity with the consumer's consent, through cookies.

Exam Probability: **Low**

44. *Answer choices:*

(see index for correct answer)

- a. Spyware
- b. BredoLab botnet

- c. SSL-Explorer: Community Edition
- d. Oulu University Secure Programming Group

Guidance: level 1

:: Transport layer protocols ::

In computer networking, the _____ is a conceptual division of methods in the layered architecture of protocols in the network stack in the Internet protocol suite and the OSI model. The protocols of this layer provide host-to-host communication services for applications. It provides services such as connection-oriented communication, reliability, flow control, and multiplexing.

Exam Probability: **Medium**

45. *Answer choices:*

(see index for correct answer)

- a. ALCAP
- b. Sinec H1
- c. Signalling Connection Control Part
- d. Transport Layer

Guidance: level 1

:: Network addressing ::

In the Internet addressing architecture, a _____ is a network that uses private IP address space. Both, the IPv4 and the IPv6 specifications define private addressing ranges. These addresses are commonly used for local area networks in residential, office, and enterprise environments. Private IP address spaces were originally defined in an effort to delay IPv4 address exhaustion.

Exam Probability: **Medium**

46. *Answer choices:*

(see index for correct answer)

- a. Naming scheme
- b. Individual Address Block
- c. Organizationally unique identifier
- d. Private network

Guidance: level 1

:: Computer data ::

In computer science, _____ is the ability to access an arbitrary element of a sequence in equal time or any datum from a population of addressable elements roughly as easily and efficiently as any other, no matter how many elements may be in the set. It is typically contrasted to sequential access.

Exam Probability: **Low**

47. *Answer choices:*

(see index for correct answer)

- a. Random access
- b. 12-bit
- c. JBOB
- d. Persistent data

Guidance: level 1

:: Information technology ::

_____ is the use of computers to store, retrieve, transmit, and manipulate data, or information, often in the context of a business or other enterprise. IT is considered to be a subset of information and communications technology . An _____ system is generally an information system, a communications system or, more specifically speaking, a computer system – including all hardware, software and peripheral equipment – operated by a limited group of users.

Exam Probability: **Medium**

48. *Answer choices:*

(see index for correct answer)

- a. Infocommunications
- b. IT as a service
- c. Toolbox.com

- d. Information technology

Guidance: level 1

:: Identity ::

A _____ is a set of connected behaviors, rights, obligations, beliefs, and norms as conceptualized by people in a social situation. It is an expected or free or continuously changing behaviour and may have a given individual social status or social position. It is vital to both functionalist and interactionist understandings of society. Social _____ posits the following about social behaviour.

Exam Probability: **High**

49. *Answer choices:*

(see index for correct answer)

- a. Gender schema theory
- b. Identity Performance
- c. Wishful Identification
- d. Ship of Theseus

Guidance: level 1

:: Internet fraud ::

_____ is the act of using a computer to take or alter electronic data, or to gain unlawful use of a computer or system. In the United States, _____ is specifically proscribed by the _____ and Abuse Act, which criminalizes computer-related acts under federal jurisdiction. Types of _____ include.

Exam Probability: **High**

50. *Answer choices:*

(see index for correct answer)

- a. Computer fraud
- b. Click fraud
- c. Pills, porn and poker
- d. Russian Business Network

Guidance: level 1

:: Hypertext ::

_____ is the process of creating, sharing, using and managing the knowledge and information of an organisation. It refers to a multidisciplinary approach to achieving organisational objectives by making the best use of knowledge.

Exam Probability: **Medium**

51. Answer choices:

(see index for correct answer)

- a. Intermedia
- b. WinPlus
- c. Adaptive educational hypermedia
- d. Knowledge management

Guidance: level 1

:: Data analysis ::

_____ is the process of discovering patterns in large data sets involving methods at the intersection of machine learning, statistics, and database systems. _____ is an interdisciplinary subfield of computer science and statistics with an overall goal to extract information from a data set and transform the information into a comprehensible structure for further use. _____ is the analysis step of the "knowledge discovery in databases" process, or KDD. Aside from the raw analysis step, it also involves database and data management aspects, data pre-processing, model and inference considerations, interestingness metrics, complexity considerations, post-processing of discovered structures, visualization, and online updating. The difference between data analysis and _____ is that data analysis is used to test models and hypotheses on the dataset, e.g., analyzing the effectiveness of a marketing campaign, regardless of the amount of data; in contrast, _____ uses machine-learning and statistical models to uncover clandestine or hidden patterns in a large volume of data.

Exam Probability: **Low**

52. *Answer choices:*

(see index for correct answer)

- a. Random mapping
- b. Visual inspection
- c. Data mining
- d. 1.96

Guidance: level 1

:: Windowing systems ::

_____ or MGR was an early windowing system originally designed and developed for Sun computers in 1984 by Stephen A. Uhler, then at Bellcore.

Exam Probability: **Medium**

53. *Answer choices:*

(see index for correct answer)

- a. Windowing system
- b. Graphical Environment Manager
- c. File Explorer
- d. Manager

Guidance: level 1

:: Software development philosophies ::

A _____ is a method or technique that has been generally accepted as superior to any alternatives because it produces results that are superior to those achieved by other means or because it has become a standard way of doing things, e.g., a standard way of complying with legal or ethical requirements.

Exam Probability: **High**

54. *Answer choices:*

(see index for correct answer)

- a. Hollywood principle
- b. Extreme programming
- c. Best practice
- d. Unix philosophy

Guidance: level 1

:: Fault-tolerant computer systems ::

Transaction processing is information processing in computer science that is divided into individual, indivisible operations called transactions. Each transaction must succeed or fail as a complete unit; it can never be only partially complete.

Exam Probability: **Medium**

55. *Answer choices:*

(see index for correct answer)

- a. Disk array
- b. Transaction processing
- c. Tandem Computers
- d. Self-stabilization

Guidance: level 1

:: Library science ::

A _____ is a curated collection of sources of information and similar resources, selected by experts and made accessible to a defined community for reference or borrowing. It provides physical or digital access to material, and may be a physical location or a virtual space, or both. A _____'s collection can include books, periodicals, newspapers, manuscripts, films, maps, prints, documents, microform, CDs, cassettes, videotapes, DVDs, Blu-ray Discs, e-books, audiobooks, databases, and other formats. Libraries range widely in size up to millions of items. In Latin and Greek, the idea of a bookcase is represented by Bibliotheca and Bibliotheke : derivatives of these mean _____ in many modern languages, e.g. French bibliothèque.

Exam Probability: **Medium**

56. *Answer choices:*

(see index for correct answer)

- a. Information grazing
- b. Digital reference
- c. Library
- d. Unshelved

Guidance: level 1

:: GPS navigation devices ::

_____ is a line of tablet computers designed, developed and marketed by Apple Inc., which run the iOS mobile operating system. The first _____ was released on April 3, 2010; the most recent _____ models are the _____, released on March 27, 2018; the fifth-generation _____ mini, released on March 18, 2019; the third-generation _____ Air, released on March 18, 2019; and the 11-inch and third-generation 12.9-inch _____ Pro, released on November 7, 2018.

Exam Probability: **High**

57. *Answer choices:*

(see index for correct answer)

- a. Nokia E72
- b. IPad
- c. Snooper
- d. Nokia 6210 Navigator

Guidance: level 1

:: Database management systems ::

A _____ is a digital database based on the relational model of data, as proposed by E. F. Codd in 1970. A software system used to maintain _____ s is a _____ management system. Virtually all _____ systems use SQL for querying and maintaining the database.

Exam Probability: **Low**

58. *Answer choices:*

(see index for correct answer)

- a. Transaction time
- b. Document-oriented database
- c. NoSQL
- d. Relational database

Guidance: level 1

:: Data management ::

A _____ , or metadata repository, as defined in the IBM Dictionary of Computing, is a "centralized repository of information about data such as meaning, relationships to other data, origin, usage, and format". Oracle defines it as a collection of tables with metadata. The term can have one of several closely related meanings pertaining to databases and database management systems .

Exam Probability: **Low**

59. *Answer choices:*
(see index for correct answer)

- a. Data auditing
- b. Project workforce management
- c. Data grid
- d. Data custodian

Guidance: level 1

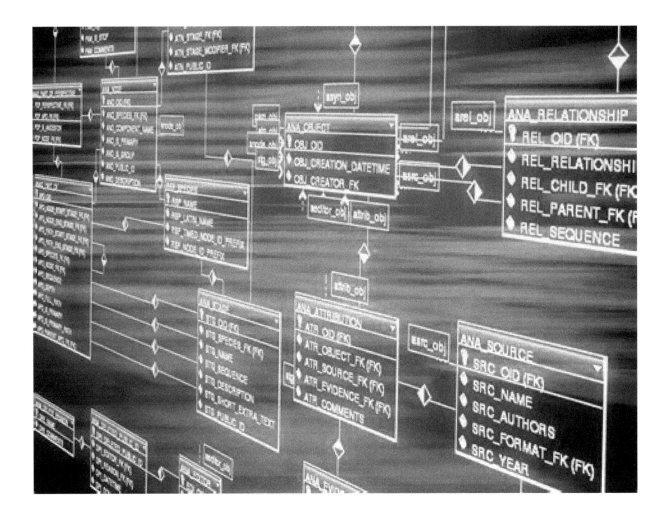

Database management

A database is an organized collection of data, generally stored and accessed electronically from a computer system. The database management system is the software that interacts with end users, applications, and the database itself to capture and analyze the data. The DBMS software additionally encompasses the core facilities provided to administer the database. The sum total of the database, the DBMS and the associated applications can be referred to as a "database system".

:: Control characters ::

_____ is the boundless three-dimensional extent in which objects and events have relative position and direction. Physical _____ is often conceived in three linear dimensions, although modern physicists usually consider it, with time, to be part of a boundless four-dimensional continuum known as _____ time. The concept of _____ is considered to be of fundamental importance to an understanding of the physical universe. However, disagreement continues between philosophers over whether it is itself an entity, a relationship between entities, or part of a conceptual framework.

Exam Probability: **Low**

1. *Answer choices:*

(see index for correct answer)

- a. Combining Grapheme Joiner
- b. Zero-width joiner
- c. Right-to-left mark
- d. Space

Guidance: level 1

:: Database constraints ::

In relational database theory, a _____ is a constraint between two sets of attributes in a relation from a database. In other words, _____ is between attributes in a relation.

Exam Probability: **Medium**

2. *Answer choices:*

(see index for correct answer)

- a. Multivalued dependency
- b. Transitive dependency
- c. Functional dependency

Guidance: level 1

:: Data analysis ::

_____ is the process of discovering patterns in large data sets involving methods at the intersection of machine learning, statistics, and database systems. _____ is an interdisciplinary subfield of computer science and statistics with an overall goal to extract information from a data set and transform the information into a comprehensible structure for further use. _____ is the analysis step of the "knowledge discovery in databases" process, or KDD. Aside from the raw analysis step, it also involves database and data management aspects, data pre-processing, model and inference considerations, interestingness metrics, complexity considerations, post-processing of discovered structures, visualization, and online updating. The difference between data analysis and _____ is that data analysis is used to test models and hypotheses on the dataset, e.g., analyzing the effectiveness of a marketing campaign, regardless of the amount of data; in contrast, _____ uses machine-learning and statistical models to uncover clandestine or hidden patterns in a large volume of data.

Exam Probability: **High**

3. *Answer choices:*

(see index for correct answer)

- a. Functional data analysis
- b. Missing data
- c. Data mining
- d. Proxy

Guidance: level 1

:: Online analytical processing ::

_____ , or OLAP , is an approach to answer multi-dimensional analytical queries swiftly in computing. OLAP is part of the broader category of business intelligence, which also encompasses relational databases, report writing and data mining. Typical applications of OLAP include business reporting for sales, marketing, management reporting, business process management , budgeting and forecasting, financial reporting and similar areas, with new applications emerging, such as agriculture. The term OLAP was created as a slight modification of the traditional database term online transaction processing .

Exam Probability: **Medium**

4. *Answer choices:*

(see index for correct answer)

- a. Dimensional Insight
- b. Online analytical processing
- c. FASMI

- d. BusinessObjects OLAP Intelligence

Guidance: level 1

:: Database management systems ::

In the relational model of databases, a _____ of a relation is a minimal superkey for that relation; that is, a set of attributes such that.

Exam Probability: **Medium**

5. *Answer choices:*

(see index for correct answer)

- a. Expression index
- b. Commit
- c. Candidate key
- d. Data hub

Guidance: level 1

:: Relational database management systems ::

Db2 is a family of data management products, including database servers, developed by IBM. They support the relational model, but in recent years, some products have been extended to support object-relational features and non-relational structures like JSON and XML. The brand name was styled as DB2 from its creation in 1983 until 2017.

Exam Probability: **Medium**

6. *Answer choices:*

(see index for correct answer)

- a. IBM DB2
- b. Database Management Library
- c. CSQL
- d. Adaptive Server Enterprise

Guidance: level 1

:: Databases ::

In databases and transaction processing, _____ is a concurrency control method that guarantees serializability. It is also the name of the resulting set of database transaction schedules. The protocol utilizes locks, applied by a transaction to data, which may block other transactions from accessing the same data during the transaction's life.

Exam Probability: **Low**

7. *Answer choices:*

(see index for correct answer)

- a. Log shipping
- b. Two-phase locking
- c. Load file
- d. Spanner

Guidance: level 1

:: Databases ::

_____ is the organisation of data according to a database model. The designer determines what data must be stored and how the data elements interrelate. With this information, they can begin to fit the data to the database model.

Exam Probability: **Low**

8. *Answer choices:*

(see index for correct answer)

- a. Hekaton
- b. Modular concurrency control
- c. Database design
- d. Springer Protocols

Guidance: level 1

:: Data security ::

In financial accounting, an _____ is any resource owned by the business. Anything tangible or intangible that can be owned or controlled to produce value and that is held by a company to produce positive economic value is an _____ . Simply stated, _____ s represent value of ownership that can be converted into cash . The balance sheet of a firm records the monetary value of the _____ s owned by that firm. It covers money and other valuables belonging to an individual or to a business.

Exam Probability: **Low**

9. *Answer choices:*

(see index for correct answer)

- a. Security convergence
- b. CronLab
- c. Alternative compensation system
- d. Asset

Guidance: level 1

:: Data structures ::

In computer science, _____ means that a group of elements is accessed in a predetermined, ordered sequence. _____ is sometimes the only way of accessing the data, for example if it is on a tape. It may also be the access method of choice, for example if all that is wanted is to process a sequence of data elements in order.

Exam Probability: **Low**

10. *Answer choices:*
(see index for correct answer)

- a. Container
- b. Search data structure
- c. Array data structure
- d. Sequential access

Guidance: level 1

:: Bioinformatics software ::

_____ is a free online bioinformatics resource developed by the Laboratory of Immunopathogenesis and Bioinformatics. All tools in the _____ Bioinformatics Resources aim to provide functional interpretation of large lists of genes derived from genomic studies, e.g. microarray and proteomics studies. _____ can be found at http:// _____ .niaid.nih.gov or http:// _____ .abcc.ncifcrf.gov

Exam Probability: **High**

11. *Answer choices:*

(see index for correct answer)

- a. TimeTree
- b. Stemloc
- c. DAVID
- d. ArrayTrack

Guidance: level 1

:: Quality control ::

_____ is a process by which entities review the quality of all factors involved in production. ISO 9000 defines _____ as "A part of quality management focused on fulfilling quality requirements".

Exam Probability: **Low**

12. *Answer choices:*

(see index for correct answer)

- a. Quality control
- b. Director of quality control
- c. AS9100
- d. Mill Test Report

Guidance: level 1

:: Programming language topics ::

In a computer language, a _____ is a word that cannot be used as an identifier, such as the name of a variable, function, or label – it is "reserved from use". This is a syntactic definition, and a _____ may have no meaning.

Exam Probability: **High**

13. *Answer choices:*

(see index for correct answer)

- a. Expressive power
- b. Humus
- c. Reserved word
- d. Exception safety

Guidance: level 1

:: Time series analysis ::

A _____ is a series of data points indexed in time order. Most commonly, a _____ is a sequence taken at successive equally spaced points in time. Thus it is a sequence of discrete-time data. Examples of _____ are heights of ocean tides, counts of sunspots, and the daily closing value of the Dow Jones Industrial Average.

Exam Probability: **Low**

14. *Answer choices:*

(see index for correct answer)

- a. Time series
- b. Trispectrum
- c. Unevenly spaced time series
- d. Autocovariance

Guidance: level 1

:: Database management systems ::

_____ is a class of relational database management systems that seek to provide the scalability of NoSQL systems for online transaction processing workloads while maintaining the ACID guarantees of a traditional database system.

Exam Probability: **Medium**

15. *Answer choices:*

(see index for correct answer)

- a. Valid time
- b. Partial index
- c. NewSQL

- d. Cursor

Guidance: level 1

:: Database management systems ::

A _____ or super-key is defined in the relational model of database organization as a set of attributes of a relation variable for which it holds that in all relations assigned to that variable, there are no two distinct tuples that have the same values for the attributes in this set. It can be defined as a set of attributes of a relation schema upon which all attributes of the schema are functionally dependent.

Exam Probability: **High**

16. *Answer choices:*

(see index for correct answer)

- a. Transaction time
- b. Referential integrity
- c. Superkey
- d. Data mart

Guidance: level 1

:: Databases ::

A _____ is a repository for persistently storing and managing collections of data which include not just repositories like databases, but also simpler store types such as simple files, emails etc.

Exam Probability: **High**

17. *Answer choices:*

(see index for correct answer)

- a. Autocommit
- b. Data store
- c. Aerospike database
- d. Elasticity

Guidance: level 1

:: Transaction processing ::

Some scenarios associate "this kind of planning" with learning "life skills". _____ s are necessary, or at least useful, in situations where individuals need to know what time they must be at a specific location to receive a specific service, and where people need to accomplish a set of goals within a set time period.

Exam Probability: **Low**

18. *Answer choices:*

(see index for correct answer)

- a. Tuxedo
- b. Schedule
- c. Same-day affirmation
- d. Transaction Workflow Innovation Standards Team

Guidance: level 1

:: Virtual reality ::

The _____ is the global system of interconnected computer networks that use the _____ protocol suite to link devices worldwide. It is a network of networks that consists of private, public, academic, business, and government networks of local to global scope, linked by a broad array of electronic, wireless, and optical networking technologies. The _____ carries a vast range of information resources and services, such as the inter-linked hypertext documents and applications of the World Wide Web, electronic mail, telephony, and file sharing.

Exam Probability: **Low**

19. *Answer choices:*

(see index for correct answer)

- a. Virtuality
- b. Surgery simulator
- c. Forterra Systems

- d. E-society

Guidance: level 1

:: Database management systems ::

A _____ is a storage location where the actual data underlying database objects can be kept. It provides a layer of abstraction between physical and logical data, and serves to allocate storage for all DBMS managed segments. Once created, a _____ can be referred to by name when creating database segments.

Exam Probability: **Low**

20. *Answer choices:*

(see index for correct answer)

- a. Row
- b. Transaction time
- c. Object-relational database
- d. Tablespace

Guidance: level 1

:: Database management systems ::

A _____ in a database is a unique identifier for either an entity in the modeled world or an object in the database. The _____ is not derived from application data, unlike a natural key which is derived from application data.

Exam Probability: **Medium**

21. *Answer choices:*

(see index for correct answer)

- a. Transaction time
- b. Database theory
- c. Surrogate key
- d. Precedence graph

Guidance: level 1

:: Sensitivity analysis ::

_____ is the study of how the uncertainty in the output of a mathematical model or system can be divided and allocated to different sources of uncertainty in its inputs. A related practice is uncertainty analysis, which has a greater focus on uncertainty quantification and propagation of uncertainty; ideally, uncertainty and _____ should be run in tandem.

Exam Probability: **Low**

22. Answer choices:

(see index for correct answer)

- a. Elementary effects method
- b. Sensitivity analysis
- c. Fourier amplitude sensitivity testing
- d. Tornado diagram

Guidance: level 1

:: Data types ::

In computer science and computer programming, a _____ or simply type is an attribute of data which tells the compiler or interpreter how the programmer intends to use the data. Most programming languages support common _____ s of real, integer and boolean. A _____ constrains the values that an expression, such as a variable or a function, might take. This _____ defines the operations that can be done on the data, the meaning of the data, and the way values of that type can be stored. A type of value from which an expression may take its value.

Exam Probability: **Medium**

23. Answer choices:

(see index for correct answer)

- a. Recursive data type
- b. Word

- c. Kind
- d. Data type

Guidance: level 1

:: Databases ::

A _____ is a server which houses a database application that provides database services to other computer programs or to computers, as defined by the client–server model. Database management systems frequently provide database-server functionality, and some database management systems rely exclusively on the client–server model for database access.

Exam Probability: **Low**

24. *Answer choices:*

(see index for correct answer)

- a. Database application
- b. Enterprise database management
- c. Database server
- d. Autocommit

Guidance: level 1

:: Online analytical processing ::

An _____ is a multi-dimensional array of data. Online analytical processing is a computer-based technique of analyzing data to look for insights. The term cube here refers to a multi-dimensional dataset, which is also sometimes called a hypercube if the number of dimensions is greater than 3.

Exam Probability: **High**

25. *Answer choices:*

(see index for correct answer)

- a. Dimensional Insight
- b. MicroStrategy
- c. OLAP cube
- d. IcCube

Guidance: level 1

:: Database management systems ::

A _____ is a subroutine available to applications that access a relational database management system. Such procedures are stored in the database data dictionary.

Exam Probability: **High**

26. *Answer choices:*

(see index for correct answer)

- a. Partition
- b. Relational calculus
- c. Stored procedure
- d. Data retrieval

Guidance: level 1

:: Data management ::

In computing, a _____ , also known as an enterprise _____ , is a system used for reporting and data analysis, and is considered a core component of business intelligence. DWs are central repositories of integrated data from one or more disparate sources. They store current and historical data in one single place that are used for creating analytical reports for workers throughout the enterprise.

Exam Probability: **Medium**

27. *Answer choices:*

(see index for correct answer)

- a. Change data capture
- b. Content format
- c. IMS VDEX
- d. Data warehouse

Guidance: level 1

:: Web development ::

A _____ is server software, or hardware dedicated to running said software, that can satisfy World Wide Web client requests. A _____ can, in general, contain one or more websites. A _____ processes incoming network requests over HTTP and several other related protocols.

Exam Probability: **Low**

28. *Answer choices:*

(see index for correct answer)

- a. Asynchronous module definition
- b. Static web page
- c. Constant Object Proportion Rendering
- d. Web server

Guidance: level 1

:: Data modeling languages ::

An _____ is a description of a type of XML document, typically expressed in terms of constraints on the structure and content of documents of that type, above and beyond the basic syntactical constraints imposed by XML itself. These constraints are generally expressed using some combination of grammatical rules governing the order of elements, Boolean predicates that the content must satisfy, data types governing the content of elements and attributes, and more specialized rules such as uniqueness and referential integrity constraints.

Exam Probability: **Low**

29. *Answer choices:*
(see index for correct answer)

- a. Data Format Description Language
- b. External Data Representation
- c. XML schema
- d. Document Structure Description

Guidance: level 1

:: Databases ::

A _____ is a computer program whose primary purpose is entering and retrieving information from a computerized database. Early examples of _____ s were accounting systems and airline reservations systems, such as SABRE, developed starting in 1957.

Exam Probability: **Low**

30. *Answer choices:*

(see index for correct answer)

- a. Single-instance storage
- b. Termcap
- c. Event condition action
- d. Aerospike database

Guidance: level 1

:: Data security ::

_____ means protecting digital data, such as those in a database, from destructive forces and from the unwanted actions of unauthorized users, such as a cyberattack or a data breach.

Exam Probability: **Low**

31. *Answer choices:*

(see index for correct answer)

- a. Extended Access Control
- b. Paper key
- c. Data security
- d. SWIPSY

Guidance: level 1

:: Transaction processing ::

_____ is the maintenance of, and the assurance of the accuracy and consistency of, data over its entire life-cycle, and is a critical aspect to the design, implementation and usage of any system which stores, processes, or retrieves data. The term is broad in scope and may have widely different meanings depending on the specific context even under the same general umbrella of computing. It is at times used as a proxy term for data quality, while data validation is a pre-requisite for _____ . _____ is the opposite of data corruption. The overall intent of any _____ technique is the same: ensure data is recorded exactly as intended and upon later retrieval, ensure the data is the same as it was when it was originally recorded. In short, _____ aims to prevent unintentional changes to information. _____ is not to be confused with data security, the discipline of protecting data from unauthorized parties.

Exam Probability: **Medium**

32. *Answer choices:*

(see index for correct answer)

- a. Blind write
- b. Thomas write rule
- c. Data integrity
- d. Teleprocessing monitor

Guidance: level 1

:: Transaction processing ::

A _____ is a database transaction in which two or more network hosts are involved. Usually, hosts provide transactional resources, while the transaction manager is responsible for creating and managing a global transaction that encompasses all operations against such resources. _____ s, as any other transactions, must have all four ACID properties, where atomicity guarantees all-or-nothing outcomes for the unit of work.

Exam Probability: **High**

33. *Answer choices:*

(see index for correct answer)

- a. Transactional memory
- b. Non-lock concurrency control
- c. Distributed transaction
- d. Pseudoconversational transaction

Guidance: level 1

:: Database management systems ::

A _____ or pillar in architecture and structural engineering is a structural element that transmits, through compression, the weight of the structure above to other structural elements below. In other words, a _____ is a compression member. The term _____ applies especially to a large round support with a capital and a base or pedestal which is made of stone, or appearing to be so. A small wooden or metal support is typically called a post, and supports with a rectangular or other non-round section are usually called piers. For the purpose of wind or earthquake engineering, _____ s may be designed to resist lateral forces. Other compression members are often termed " _____ s" because of the similar stress conditions. _____ s are frequently used to support beams or arches on which the upper parts of walls or ceilings rest. In architecture, " _____ " refers to such a structural element that also has certain proportional and decorative features. A _____ might also be a decorative element not needed for structural purposes; many _____ s are "engaged", that is to say form part of a wall.

Exam Probability: **Medium**

34. *Answer choices:*
(see index for correct answer)

- a. Federated database system
- b. Column
- c. Object-based spatial database
- d. Big data

Guidance: level 1

:: Formal languages ::

In computer text processing, a _____ is a system for annotating a document in a way that is syntactically distinguishable from the text. The idea and terminology evolved from the "marking up" of paper manuscripts, i.e., the revision instructions by editors, traditionally written with a red or blue pencil on authors' manuscripts. In digital media this "blue pencil instruction text" was replaced by tags, which indicate what the parts of the document are, rather than details of how they might be shown on some display. This lets authors avoid formatting every instance of the same kind of thing redundantly . It also avoids the specification of fonts and dimensions, which may not apply to many users .

Exam Probability: **Low**

35. *Answer choices:*

(see index for correct answer)

- a. Concatenation
- b. Free monoid
- c. Markup language
- d. Indexed grammar

Guidance: level 1

:: Database management systems ::

A _____ is a digital database based on the relational model of data, as proposed by E. F. Codd in 1970.A software system used to maintain _____ s is a _____ management system . Virtually all _____ systems use SQL for querying and maintaining the database.

Exam Probability: **Low**

36. *Answer choices:*

(see index for correct answer)

- a. Block contention
- b. Database tuning
- c. Expression index
- d. In-memory database

Guidance: level 1

:: Abstraction ::

_____ is the state or quality of being simple. Something easy to understand or explain seems simple, in contrast to something complicated. Alternatively, as Herbert A. Simon suggests, something is simple or complex depending on the way we choose to describe it. In some uses, the label " _____ " can imply beauty, purity, or clarity. In other cases, the term may occur with negative connotations to suggest, a deficit or insufficiency of nuance or of complexity of a thing, relative to what one supposes as required.

Exam Probability: **High**

37. *Answer choices:*

(see index for correct answer)

- a. Meta

- b. Hypostatic abstraction
- c. Continuous predicate
- d. Maladaptive daydreaming

Guidance: level 1

:: Data management ::

_____ is an object-oriented program and library developed by CERN. It was originally designed for particle physics data analysis and contains several features specific to this field, but it is also used in other applications such as astronomy and data mining. The latest release is 6.16.00, as of 2018-11-14.

Exam Probability: **Low**

38. *Answer choices:*
(see index for correct answer)

- a. Data room
- b. Data Reference Model
- c. Data management plan
- d. ROOT

Guidance: level 1

:: Database management systems ::

_____ is a property of data stating that all of its references are valid. In the context of relational databases, it requires that if a value of one attribute of a relation references a value of another attribute, then the referenced value must exist.

Exam Probability: **Medium**

39. *Answer choices:*

(see index for correct answer)

- a. ANSI-SPARC Architecture
- b. Associative model of data
- c. Quorum
- d. Database transaction

Guidance: level 1

:: Database stubs ::

_____, also known as rogue data, are inaccurate, incomplete or inconsistent data, especially in a computer system or database.

Exam Probability: **Low**

40. *Answer choices:*

(see index for correct answer)

- a. PsycCRITIQUES
- b. Effective date
- c. Oracle Real Application Testing
- d. USDA National Nutrient Database

Guidance: level 1

:: Local area networks ::

A _____ is a computer network that interconnects computers within a limited area such as a residence, school, laboratory, university campus or office building. By contrast, a wide area network not only covers a larger geographic distance, but also generally involves leased telecommunication circuits.

Exam Probability: **Low**

41. *Answer choices:*

(see index for correct answer)

- a. Subinterface
- b. Distributed-queue dual-bus
- c. Fiber Distributed Data Interface
- d. Sun Fire Link

Guidance: level 1

:: Database management systems ::

A data definition or data description language is a syntax similar to a computer programming language for defining data structures, especially database schemas. DDL statements create, modify, and remove database objects such as tables, indexes, and users. Common DDL statements are CREATE, ALTER, and DROP

Exam Probability: **High**

42. *Answer choices:*

(see index for correct answer)

- a. Stored procedure
- b. Transaction log
- c. Types of DBMS
- d. Data Definition Language

Guidance: level 1

:: Computer file systems ::

An _____ is a function of a mainframe operating system that enables access to data on disk, tape or other external devices. They were introduced in 1963 in IBM OS/360 operating system. _____ s provide an application programming interface for programmers to transfer data to or from device, and could be compared to device drivers in non-mainframe operating systems, but typically provide a greater level of functionality.

Exam Probability: **High**

43. *Answer choices:*

(see index for correct answer)

- a. Virtual folder
- b. File grooming
- c. Pattern file
- d. Access method

Guidance: level 1

:: Data modeling ::

A _____ is an abstract model that organizes elements of data and standardizes how they relate to one another and to properties of the real world entities. For instance, a _____ may specify that the data element representing a car be composed of a number of other elements which, in turn, represent the color and size of the car and define its owner.

Exam Probability: **Medium**

44. *Answer choices:*

(see index for correct answer)

- a. Standard user model
- b. Data efficacy

- c. Data model
- d. NORMA

Guidance: level 1

:: SQL ::

_____ is a method of combining the computing power of a programming language and the database manipulation capabilities of SQL. _____ statements are SQL statements written inline with the program source code, of the host language. The _____ statements are parsed by an _____ preprocessor and replaced by host-language calls to a code library. The output from the preprocessor is then compiled by the host compiler. This allows programmers to embed SQL statements in programs written in any number of languages such as C/C++, COBOL and Fortran. This differs from SQL-derived programming languages that don't go through discrete preprocessors, such as PL/SQL and T-SQL.

Exam Probability: **Low**

45. *Answer choices:*

(see index for correct answer)

- a. PL/pgSQL
- b. Embedded SQL
- c. Database Console Commands
- d. SQL:2003

Guidance: level 1

:: E-commerce ::

_____ is the activity of buying or selling of products on online services or over the Internet. Electronic commerce draws on technologies such as mobile commerce, electronic funds transfer, supply chain management, Internet marketing, online transaction processing, electronic data interchange , inventory management systems, and automated data collection systems.

Exam Probability: **Low**

46. *Answer choices:*

(see index for correct answer)

- a. E-commerce
- b. RapidBuyr
- c. Customer to customer
- d. PapiNet

Guidance: level 1

:: Databases ::

In concurrency control of databases, transaction processing, and various transactional applications, both centralized and distributed, a transaction schedule is serializable if its outcome is equal to the outcome of its transactions executed serially, i.e. without overlapping in time. Transactions are normally executed concurrently, since this is the most efficient way. _____ is the major correctness criterion for concurrent transactions` executions. It is considered the highest level of isolation between transactions, and plays an essential role in concurrency control. As such it is supported in all general purpose database systems. Strong strict two-phase locking is a popular _____ mechanism utilized in most of the database systems since their early days in the 1970s.

Exam Probability: **Low**

47. *Answer choices:*

(see index for correct answer)

- a. Serializability
- b. Data item
- c. Identity column
- d. Data redundancy

Guidance: level 1

:: Bit data structures ::

In computing, a _____ is a mapping from some domain to bits. It is also called a bit array or _____ index.

Exam Probability: **High**

48. *Answer choices:*

(see index for correct answer)

- a. Bit field
- b. Bitmap
- c. Bit plane

Guidance: level 1

:: Unix programming tools ::

_____ is a family of two high-level, general-purpose, interpreted, dynamic programming languages. " _____ " usually refers to _____ 5, but it may also refer to its redesigned "sister language", _____ 6.

Exam Probability: **Low**

49. *Answer choices:*

(see index for correct answer)

- a. Lipog
- b. Strip
- c. Makedepend
- d. FreeMat

Guidance: level 1

:: Data analysis ::

In statistics, the _____ is a measure that is used to quantify the amount of variation or dispersion of a set of data values. A low _____ indicates that the data points tend to be close to the mean of the set, while a high _____ indicates that the data points are spread out over a wider range of values.

Exam Probability: **High**

50. *Answer choices:*

(see index for correct answer)

- a. Crosstab
- b. Correspondence analysis
- c. Power transform
- d. Data definition specification

Guidance: level 1

:: Data management ::

The _____ of a database system is its structure described in a formal language supported by the database management system. The term "schema" refers to the organization of data as a blueprint of how the database is constructed. The formal definition of a _____ is a set of formulas called integrity constraints imposed on a database. These integrity constraints ensure compatibility between parts of the schema. All constraints are expressible in the same language. A database can be considered a structure in realization of the database language. The states of a created conceptual schema are transformed into an explicit mapping, the _____. This describes how real-world entities are modeled in the database.

Exam Probability: **Low**

51. *Answer choices:*

(see index for correct answer)

- a. Vector-field consistency
- b. Learning object
- c. Geospatial metadata
- d. Microsoft SQL Server Master Data Services

Guidance: level 1

:: Computer memory ::

_____ is the complex cognitive process of decoding symbols to derive meaning. It is a form of language processing.

Exam Probability: **Medium**

52. *Answer choices:*

(see index for correct answer)

- a. IBM 2361 Large Capacity Storage
- b. EEPROM
- c. Reading
- d. Molecular memory

Guidance: level 1

:: Scripting languages ::

_____ is an Active Scripting language developed by Microsoft that is modeled on Visual Basic. It allows Microsoft Windows system administrators to generate powerful tools for managing computers with error handling, subroutines, and other advanced programming constructs. It can give the user complete control over many aspects of their computing environment.

Exam Probability: **High**

53. *Answer choices:*

(see index for correct answer)

- a. ECMAScript
- b. JScript

Guidance: level 1

:: Holism ::

_____ characterises the behaviour of a system or model whose components interact in multiple ways and follow local rules, meaning there is no reasonable higher instruction to define the various possible interactions.

Exam Probability: **Low**

54. *Answer choices:*
(see index for correct answer)

- a. Complexity
- b. Process philosophy
- c. Modular programming
- d. Theory of Colours

Guidance: level 1

:: Database management systems ::

A _____ is a structure / access pattern specific to data warehouse environments, used to retrieve client-facing data. The _____ is a subset of the data warehouse and is usually oriented to a specific business line or team. Whereas data warehouses have an enterprise-wide depth, the information in _____ s pertains to a single department. In some deployments, each department or business unit is considered the owner of its _____ including all the hardware, software and data. This enables each department to isolate the use, manipulation and development of their data. In other deployments where conformed dimensions are used, this business unit ownership will not hold true for shared dimensions like customer, product, etc.

Exam Probability: **High**

55. *Answer choices:*

(see index for correct answer)

- a. Secondary database server
- b. View
- c. Temporal database
- d. Data mart

Guidance: level 1

:: Database security ::

_____ is a key issue in a Real time, we know that all our data is some where store in database. _____ concerns the use of a broad range of information security controls to protect databases against compromises of their confidentiality, integrity and availability. It involves various types or categories of controls, such as technical, procedural/administrative and physical. _____ is a specialist topic within the broader realms of computer security, information security and risk management.

Exam Probability: **Medium**

56. *Answer choices:*

(see index for correct answer)

- a. Negative database
- b. Database forensics
- c. Database security

Guidance: level 1

:: Network performance ::

_____ is the improvement of system performance. Typically in computer systems, the motivation for such activity is called a performance problem, which can be either real or anticipated. Most systems will respond to increased load with some degree of decreasing performance. A system's ability to accept higher load is called scalability, and modifying a system to handle a higher load is synonymous to _____ .

Exam Probability: **Low**

57. *Answer choices:*

(see index for correct answer)

- a. NetEqualizer
- b. Bandwidth guaranteed polling
- c. Service assurance
- d. Bit error rate

Guidance: level 1

:: Database management systems ::

A _____ database provides a mechanism for storage and retrieval of data that is modeled in means other than the tabular relations used in relational databases. Such databases have existed since the late 1960s, but did not obtain the "_____" moniker until a surge of popularity in the early 21st century, triggered by the needs of Web 2.0 companies. _____ databases are increasingly used in big data and real-time web applications. _____ systems are also sometimes called "Not only SQL" to emphasize that they may support SQL-like query languages, or sit alongside SQL database in a polyglot persistence architecture.

Exam Probability: **High**

58. *Answer choices:*

(see index for correct answer)

- a. Candidate key
- b. Microsoft SQL Server
- c. Triplestore
- d. XML database

Guidance: level 1

:: Database management systems ::

_____ is a proprietary multi-model database management system produced and marketed by Oracle Corporation.

Exam Probability: **Medium**

59. *Answer choices:*
(see index for correct answer)

- a. Federated database system
- b. Database model
- c. Oracle Database
- d. Relational algebra

Guidance: level 1

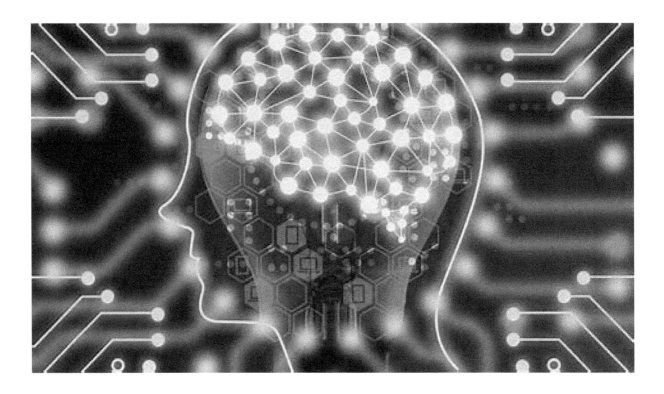

Artificial intelligence

Artificial intelligence, sometimes called machine intelligence, is intelligence demonstrated by machines, in contrast to the natural intelligence displayed by humans and other animals. In computer science AI research is defined as the study of "intelligent agents": any device that perceives its environment and takes actions that maximize its chance of successfully achieving its goals.

:: Measurement ::

An _____ is an action which is inaccurate or incorrect. In some usages, an _____ is synonymous with a mistake. In statistics, "_____" refers to the difference between the value which has been computed and the correct value. An _____ could result in failure or in a deviation from the intended performance or behaviour.

Exam Probability: **High**

1. *Answer choices:*

(see index for correct answer)

- a. Observational error
- b. Standard conditions for temperature and pressure
- c. Error
- d. Anthropic units

Guidance: level 1

:: Logic programming ::

_____ is a type of programming paradigm which is largely based on formal logic. Any program written in a _____ language is a set of sentences in logical form, expressing facts and rules about some problem domain. Major _____ language families include Prolog, answer set programming and Datalog. In all of these languages, rules are written in the form of clauses.

Exam Probability: **Medium**

2. *Answer choices:*

(see index for correct answer)

- a. Stable model semantics
- b. Functional logic programming
- c. Cut
- d. Autoepistemic logic

Guidance: level 1

:: Dynamical systems ::

In mathematics and science, a _____ is a system in which the change of the output is not proportional to the change of the input. Nonlinear problems are of interest to engineers, biologists, physicists, mathematicians, and many other scientists because most systems are inherently nonlinear in nature. Nonlinear dynamical systems, describing changes in variables over time, may appear chaotic, unpredictable, or counterintuitive, contrasting with much simpler linear systems.

Exam Probability: **Low**

3. *Answer choices:*

(see index for correct answer)

- a. Variable structure system
- b. Fractional-order system
- c. Nonlinear system

- d. Langevin dynamics

Guidance: level 1

:: Data analysis ::

In statistics, an _____ is a data point that differs significantly from other observations. An _____ may be due to variability in the measurement or it may indicate experimental error; the latter are sometimes excluded from the data set. An _____ can cause serious problems in statistical analyses.

Exam Probability: **Medium**

4. *Answer choices:*
(see index for correct answer)

- a. Outlier
- b. Data analysis
- c. Political forecasting
- d. Data definition specification

Guidance: level 1

:: Natural language processing ::

_____ is a technique in natural language processing, in particular distributional semantics, of analyzing relationships between a set of documents and the terms they contain by producing a set of concepts related to the documents and terms. LSA assumes that words that are close in meaning will occur in similar pieces of text. A matrix containing word counts per paragraph is constructed from a large piece of text and a mathematical technique called singular value decomposition is used to reduce the number of rows while preserving the similarity structure among columns. Paragraphs are then compared by taking the cosine of the angle between the two vectors formed by any two columns. Values close to 1 represent very similar paragraphs while values close to 0 represent very dissimilar paragraphs.

Exam Probability: **High**

5. *Answer choices:*

(see index for correct answer)

- a. Attempto Controlled English
- b. Latent semantic mapping
- c. Latent semantic analysis
- d. Word-sense disambiguation

Guidance: level 1

:: Estimation of densities ::

In probability and statistics, _____ is the construction of an estimate, based on observed data, of an unobservable underlying probability density function. The unobservable density function is thought of as the density according to which a large population is distributed; the data are usually thought of as a random sample from that population.

Exam Probability: **Medium**

6. *Answer choices:*
(see index for correct answer)

- a. Kernel density estimation
- b. Density estimation
- c. Cluster-weighted modeling

Guidance: level 1

:: Measurement ::

_____ is a property that can exist as a multitude or magnitude. Quantities can be compared in terms of "more", "less", or "equal", or by assigning a numerical value in terms of a unit of measurement. _____ is among the basic classes of things along with quality, substance, change, and relation. Some quantities are such by their inner nature , while others are functioning as states of things such as heavy and light, long and short, broad and narrow, small and great, or much and little.

Exam Probability: **High**

7. Answer choices:

(see index for correct answer)

- a. Laser Doppler velocimetry
- b. Guaranteed minimum value
- c. Bite force quotient
- d. Quantity

Guidance: level 1

:: Logic in computer science ::

In mathematical logic and logic programming, a _____ is a logical formula of a particular rule-like form which gives it useful properties for use in logic programming, formal specification, and model theory. _____ s are named for the logician Alfred Horn, who first pointed out their significance in 1951.

Exam Probability: **Low**

8. Answer choices:

(see index for correct answer)

- a. Geometry of interaction
- b. Bunched logic
- c. Twelf
- d. Horn clause

Guidance: level 1

:: Classification algorithms ::

In machine learning, the _____ is an algorithm for supervised learning of binary classifiers. A binary classifier is a function which can decide whether or not an input, represented by a vector of numbers, belongs to some specific class. It is a type of linear classifier, i.e. a classification algorithm that makes its predictions based on a linear predictor function combining a set of weights with the feature vector.

Exam Probability: **Medium**

9. *Answer choices:*
(see index for correct answer)

- a. Kernel methods
- b. BrownBoost
- c. Linear classifier
- d. LogitBoost

Guidance: level 1

:: Computational statistics ::

_____s or Sequential Monte Carlo methods are a set of Monte Carlo algorithms used to solve filtering problems arising in signal processing and Bayesian statistical inference. The filtering problem consists of estimating the internal states in dynamical systems when partial observations are made, and random perturbations are present in the sensors as well as in the dynamical system. The objective is to compute the posterior distributions of the states of some Markov process, given some noisy and partial observations. The term "_____s" was first coined in 1996 by Del Moral in reference to mean field interacting particle methods used in fluid mechanics since the beginning of the 1960s. The terminology "sequential Monte Carlo" was proposed by Liu and Chen in 1998.

Exam Probability: **High**

10. *Answer choices:*

(see index for correct answer)

- a. Particle filter
- b. Auxiliary particle filter
- c. Bayesian inference using Gibbs sampling
- d. Continuity correction

Guidance: level 1

:: Classification algorithms ::

In a statistical-classification problem with two classes, a _____ or decision surface is a hypersurface that partitions the underlying vector space into two sets, one for each class. The classifier will classify all the points on one side of the _____ as belonging to one class and all those on the other side as belonging to the other class.

Exam Probability: **Low**

11. *Answer choices:*

(see index for correct answer)

- a. Decision boundary
- b. Linear classifier
- c. ALOPEX
- d. IDistance

Guidance: level 1

:: Randomness ::

In probability and statistics, a _____ , random quantity, aleatory variable, or stochastic variable is described informally as a variable whose values depend on outcomes of a random phenomenon. The formal mathematical treatment of _____ s is a topic in probability theory. In that context, a _____ is understood as a measurable function defined on a sample space whose outcomes are typically real numbers.

Exam Probability: **Low**

12. Answer choices:

(see index for correct answer)

- a. Algorithmically random sequence
- b. Random compact set
- c. Random number table
- d. Random variable

Guidance: level 1

:: Theoretical computer science ::

In computer science, _____ is a subfield of artificial intelligence devoted to studying the design and analysis of machine learning algorithms.

Exam Probability: **High**

13. Answer choices:

(see index for correct answer)

- a. Algorithm
- b. Peptide computing
- c. Correctness
- d. Computational learning theory

Guidance: level 1

:: Search algorithms ::

In computer science, _____ is a heuristic search algorithm that explores a graph by expanding the most promising node in a limited set. _____ is an optimization of best-first search that reduces its memory requirements. Best-first search is a graph search which orders all partial solutions according to some heuristic. But in _____ , only a predetermined number of best partial solutions are kept as candidates. It is thus a greedy algorithm.

Exam Probability: **High**

14. *Answer choices:*

(see index for correct answer)

- a. Range Minimum Query
- b. Beam search
- c. Bidirectional search
- d. Uniform-cost search

Guidance: level 1

:: Artificial intelligence ::

The _____ is an annual competition in artificial intelligence that awards prizes to the computer programs considered by the judges to be the most human-like. The format of the competition is that of a standard Turing test. In each round, a human judge simultaneously holds textual conversations with a computer program and a human being via computer. Based upon the responses, the judge must decide which is which.

Exam Probability: **High**

15. *Answer choices:*

(see index for correct answer)

- a. Intelligent personal assistant
- b. Model-based reasoning
- c. Intelligent Water Drops algorithm
- d. Loebner Prize

Guidance: level 1

:: Problem solving ::

A _____ technique, often called simply a _____, is any approach to problem solving or self-discovery that employs a practical method, not guaranteed to be optimal, perfect, logical, or rational, but instead sufficient for reaching an immediate goal. Where finding an optimal solution is impossible or impractical, _____ methods can be used to speed up the process of finding a satisfactory solution. _____ s can be mental shortcuts that ease the cognitive load of making a decision. Examples that employ _____ s include using a rule of thumb, an educated guess, an intuitive judgment, a guesstimate, profiling, or common sense.

Exam Probability: **Low**

16. *Answer choices:*

(see index for correct answer)

- a. Epiphany
- b. Collective Induction
- c. Heuristic
- d. Problem finding

Guidance: level 1

:: Automatic identification and data capture ::

_____ or optical character reader, often abbreviated as OCR, is the mechanical or electronic conversion of images of typed, handwritten or printed text into machine-encoded text, whether from a scanned document, a photo of a document, a scene-photo or from subtitle text superimposed on an image.

Exam Probability: **High**

17. *Answer choices:*

(see index for correct answer)

- a. Psion Teklogix
- b. Intelligent character recognition
- c. Optical character recognition
- d. Mobile computing

Guidance: level 1

:: Feature detection ::

_____ includes a variety of mathematical methods that aim at identifying points in a digital image at which the image brightness changes sharply or, more formally, has discontinuities. The points at which image brightness changes sharply are typically organized into a set of curved line segments termed edges. The same problem of finding discontinuities in one-dimensional signals is known as step detection and the problem of finding signal discontinuities over time is known as change detection. _____ is a fundamental tool in image processing, machine vision and computer vision, particularly in the areas of feature detection and feature extraction.

Exam Probability: **Low**

18. *Answer choices:*

(see index for correct answer)

- a. Histogram of oriented gradients
- b. Edgel
- c. Edge detection
- d. Kirsch operator

Guidance: level 1

:: Machine learning algorithms ::

_____ algorithms are a family of methods used to efficiently train artificial neural networks following a gradient descent approach that exploits the chain rule. The main feature of _____ is its iterative, recursive and efficient method for calculating the weights updates to improve in the network until it is able to perform the task for which it is being trained. It is closely related to the Gauss–Newton algorithm.

Exam Probability: **Medium**

19. *Answer choices:*
(see index for correct answer)

- a. Quadratic unconstrained binary optimization
- b. Constructing skill trees
- c. Sparse PCA
- d. Backpropagation

Guidance: level 1

:: Optimization algorithms and methods ::

_____ is an algorithm design paradigm for discrete and combinatorial optimization problems, as well as mathematical optimization. A branch-and-bound algorithm consists of a systematic enumeration of candidate solutions by means of state space search: the set of candidate solutions is thought of as forming a rooted tree with the full set at the root. The algorithm explores branches of this tree, which represent subsets of the solution set. Before enumerating the candidate solutions of a branch, the branch is checked against upper and lower estimated bounds on the optimal solution, and is discarded if it cannot produce a better solution than the best one found so far by the algorithm.

Exam Probability: **Low**

20. *Answer choices:*

(see index for correct answer)

- a. Tabu search
- b. Augmented Lagrangian method
- c. Random search
- d. Branch and bound

Guidance: level 1

:: Artificial intelligence ::

In computer science, _____ , sometimes called machine intelligence, is intelligence demonstrated by machines, in contrast to the natural intelligence displayed by humans and animals. Colloquially, the term " _____ " is used to describe machines that mimic "cognitive" functions that humans associate with other human minds, such as "learning" and "problem solving".

Exam Probability: **Low**

21. *Answer choices:*

(see index for correct answer)

- a. Artificial intelligence
- b. Herbert Gelernter
- c. Percept sequence
- d. Legal expert system

Guidance: level 1

:: Artificial intelligence ::

_____ s are a family of formal knowledge representation languages. Many DLs are more expressive than propositional logic but less expressive than first-order logic. In contrast to the latter, the core reasoning problems for DLs are decidable, and efficient decision procedures have been designed and implemented for these problems. There are general, spatial, temporal, spatiotemporal, and fuzzy descriptions logics, and each _____ features a different balance between DL expressivity and reasoning complexity by supporting different sets of mathematical constructors.

Exam Probability: **Low**

22. *Answer choices:*

(see index for correct answer)

- a. Description logic
- b. Distributed artificial intelligence
- c. Darwin machine
- d. Rule-based system

Guidance: level 1

:: Monte Carlo methods ::

In statistics, _____ is a general technique for estimating properties of a particular distribution, while only having samples generated from a different distribution than the distribution of interest. It is related to umbrella sampling in computational physics. Depending on the application, the term may refer to the process of sampling from this alternative distribution, the process of inference, or both.

Exam Probability: **Low**

23. *Answer choices:*

(see index for correct answer)

- a. Variance reduction
- b. Importance sampling

- c. Auxiliary field Monte Carlo
- d. Wolff algorithm

Guidance: level 1

:: Artificial intelligence ::

Symbolic artificial intelligence is the term for the collection of all methods in artificial intelligence research that are based on high-level "symbolic" representations of problems, logic and search. Symbolic AI was the dominant paradigm of AI research from the mid-1950s until the late 1980s.

Exam Probability: **High**

24. *Answer choices:*

(see index for correct answer)

- a. GOFAI
- b. Stochastic diffusion search
- c. DAYDREAMER
- d. Expert system

Guidance: level 1

:: Virtual reality ::

_____ is the mathematical process of recovering the movements of an object in the world from some other data, such as a film of those movements, or a film of the world as seen by a camera which is itself making those movements. This is useful in robotics and in film animation.

Exam Probability: **Low**

25. *Answer choices:*

(see index for correct answer)

- a. Inverse kinematics
- b. Lifelike experience
- c. Next Limit Technologies
- d. Virtual world

Guidance: level 1

:: Knowledge representation ::

A _____, or frame network is a knowledge base that represents semantic relations between concepts in a network. This is often used as a form of knowledge representation. It is a directed or undirected graph consisting of vertices, which represent concepts, and edges, which represent semantic relations between concepts, mapping or connecting semantic fields.

Exam Probability: **Medium**

26. *Answer choices:*

(see index for correct answer)

- a. Semantic network
- b. Pretext
- c. Enaction
- d. Darwin Core Archive

Guidance: level 1

:: Trees (data structures) ::

In computing, tree data structures, and game theory, the _____ is the number of children at each node, the outdegree. If this value is not uniform, an average _____ can be calculated.

Exam Probability: **Low**

27. *Answer choices:*

(see index for correct answer)

- a. Tree homomorphism
- b. C-trie
- c. H tree
- d. Hyperbolic tree

Guidance: level 1

:: Binary operations ::

Logical consequence is a fundamental concept in logic, which describes the relationship between statements that hold true when one statement logically follows from one or more statements. A valid logical argument is one in which the conclusion is entailed by the premises, because the conclusion is the consequence of the premises. The philosophical analysis of logical consequence involves the questions: In what sense does a conclusion follow from its premises and What does it mean for a conclusion to be a consequence of premises All of philosophical logic is meant to provide accounts of the nature of logical consequence and the nature of logical truth.

Exam Probability: **High**

28. *Answer choices:*

(see index for correct answer)

- a. Entailment
- b. symmetric difference
- c. subtraction

Guidance: level 1

:: Matrices ::

In mathematics, the _____ or Hessian is a square matrix of second-order partial derivatives of a scalar-valued function, or scalar field. It describes the local curvature of a function of many variables. The _____ was developed in the 19th century by the German mathematician Ludwig Otto Hesse and later named after him. Hesse originally used the term "functional determinants".

Exam Probability: **Medium**

29. *Answer choices:*

(see index for correct answer)

- a. Hessian matrix
- b. Arrowhead matrix
- c. Birkhoff factorization
- d. Z-matrix

Guidance: level 1

:: Decision theory ::

_____ is a negative conscious and emotional reaction to one's personal decision-making, a choice resulting in action or inaction. _____ is related to perceived opportunity. Its intensity varies over time after the decision, in regard to action versus inaction, and in regard to self-control at a particular age. The self-recrimination which comes with _____ is thought to spur corrective action and adaptation. In Western societies adults have the highest _____ s regarding choices of their education.

Exam Probability: **Low**

30. *Answer choices:*

(see index for correct answer)

- a. Consensus-seeking decision-making
- b. Prospect theory
- c. Ambiguity aversion
- d. Stochastic dominance

Guidance: level 1

:: Semantic Web ::

The _____ is an extension of the World Wide Web through standards by the World Wide Web Consortium . The standards promote common data formats and exchange protocols on the Web, most fundamentally the Resource Description Framework . According to the W3C, "The _____ provides a common framework that allows data to be shared and reused across application, enterprise, and community boundaries". The _____ is therefore regarded as an integrator across different content, information applications and systems.

Exam Probability: **High**

31. *Answer choices:*

(see index for correct answer)

- a. Adenine

- b. Microdata
- c. SSWAP
- d. Regator

Guidance: level 1

:: Bayesian networks ::

A _____ is a Bayesian network which relates variables to each other over adjacent time steps. This is often called a Two-Timeslice BN because it says that at any point in time T, the value of a variable can be calculated from the internal regressors and the immediate prior value . DBNs were developed by Paul Dagum in the early 1990s at Stanford University's Section on Medical Informatics. Dagum developed DBNs to unify and extend traditional linear state-space models such as Kalman filters, linear and normal forecasting models such as ARMA and simple dependency models such as hidden Markov models into a general probabilistic representation and inference mechanism for arbitrary nonlinear and non-normal time-dependent domains.

Exam Probability: **Medium**

32. *Answer choices:*
(see index for correct answer)

- a. Dynamic Bayesian network
- b. Latent variable
- c. Variational message passing
- d. Influence diagram

Guidance: level 1

:: Classical logic ::

First-order logic—also known as _____ and first-order predicate calculus—is a collection of formal systems used in mathematics, philosophy, linguistics, and computer science. First-order logic uses quantified variables over non-logical objects and allows the use of sentences that contain variables, so that rather than propositions such as Socrates is a man one can have expressions in the form "there exists x such that x is Socrates and x is a man" and there exists is a quantifier while x is a variable. This distinguishes it from propositional logic, which does not use quantifiers or relations; in this sense, propositional logic is the foundation of first-order logic.

Exam Probability: **Medium**

33. *Answer choices:*

(see index for correct answer)

- a. Law of noncontradiction
- b. Principle of explosion
- c. Modus tollens
- d. Law of excluded middle

Guidance: level 1

:: Dynamical systems ::

In the theory of discrete dynamical systems, a _____ is the set of all possible configurations of a system. For example, a system in queueing theory defining the number of customers in a line would have _____ . _____ s can be either infinite or finite. An example of a finite _____ is that of the toy problem Vacuum World, in which there are a limited set of configurations that the vacuum and dirt can be in.

Exam Probability: **High**

34. *Answer choices:*

(see index for correct answer)

- a. Method of averaging
- b. State space
- c. Shadowing lemma
- d. Equilibrium point

Guidance: level 1

:: History of artificial intelligence ::

The _____ was a hypothetical computer program, proposed by John McCarthy in his 1958 paper "Programs with Common Sense". It was probably the first proposal to use logic to represent information in a computer and not just as the subject matter of another program. It may also have been the first paper to propose common sense reasoning ability as the key to artificial intelligence. In his paper, McCarthy advocated.

Exam Probability: **Medium**

35. *Answer choices:*

(see index for correct answer)

- a. LIFER/LADDER
- b. Advice taker
- c. Donald Michie
- d. AI winter

Guidance: level 1

:: Imagination ::

A _____ is a proposed explanation for a phenomenon. For a _____ to be a scientific _____ , the scientific method requires that one can test it. Scientists generally base scientific hypotheses on previous observations that cannot satisfactorily be explained with the available scientific theories. Even though the words " _____ " and "theory" are often used synonymously, a scientific _____ is not the same as a scientific theory. A working _____ is a provisionally accepted _____ proposed for further research, in a process beginning with an educated guess or thought.

Exam Probability: **High**

36. *Answer choices:*

(see index for correct answer)

- a. The Imp of the Perverse
- b. Thought experiment
- c. Hypothesis
- d. Fantasy

Guidance: level 1

:: String similarity measures ::

In information theory, the _____ between two strings of equal length is the number of positions at which the corresponding symbols are different. In other words, it measures the minimum number of substitutions required to change one string into the other, or the minimum number of errors that could have transformed one string into the other. In a more general context, the _____ is one of several string metrics for measuring the edit distance between two sequences. It is named after the American mathematician Richard Hamming.

Exam Probability: **Low**

37. *Answer choices:*

(see index for correct answer)

- a. Edit distance
- b. String metric
- c. Hamming distance
- d. Lee distance

Guidance: level 1

:: Graphical models ::

_____ , also known as sum-product message passing, is a message-passing algorithm for performing inference on graphical models, such as Bayesian networks and Markov random fields. It calculates the marginal distribution for each unobserved node, conditional on any observed nodes. _____ is commonly used in artificial intelligence and information theory and has demonstrated empirical success in numerous applications including low-density parity-check codes, turbo codes, free energy approximation, and satisfiability.

Exam Probability: **Low**

38. *Answer choices:*

(see index for correct answer)

- a. M-separation
- b. Ancestral graph
- c. Variable elimination
- d. Belief propagation

Guidance: level 1

:: Statistical mechanics ::

In statistical mechanics, the _____ , a generalization of the Ising model, is a model of interacting spins on a crystalline lattice. By studying the _____ , one may gain insight into the behaviour of ferromagnets and certain other phenomena of solid-state physics. The strength of the _____ is not so much that it models these physical systems well; it is rather that the one-dimensional case is exactly solvable, and that it has a rich mathematical formulation that has been studied extensively.

Exam Probability: **High**

39. *Answer choices:*

(see index for correct answer)

- a. Potts model
- b. Entropy of mixing
- c. KT
- d. Thermal quantum field theory

Guidance: level 1

:: Search algorithms ::

In computer science, a _____ is any algorithm which solves the search problem, namely, to retrieve information stored within some data structure, or calculated in the search space of a problem domain, either with discrete or continuous values. Specific applications of _____ s include.

Exam Probability: **Low**

40. *Answer choices:*

(see index for correct answer)

- a. Search algorithm
- b. Uniform binary search
- c. Hash value
- d. Deducting Search Algorithm

Guidance: level 1

:: Artificial intelligence ::

In computer science, a _____ is used to store and manipulate knowledge to interpret information in a useful way. It is often used in artificial intelligence applications and research.

Exam Probability: **High**

41. *Answer choices:*

(see index for correct answer)

- a. Rule-based system
- b. Bees algorithm
- c. Iris
- d. Psychology of reasoning

Guidance: level 1

:: Mathematical optimization ::

The method of _____ is a standard approach in regression analysis to approximate the solution of overdetermined systems, i.e., sets of equations in which there are more equations than unknowns. "_____" means that the overall solution minimizes the sum of the squares of the residuals made in the results of every single equation.

Exam Probability: **High**

42. *Answer choices:*

(see index for correct answer)

- a. Least squares
- b. Discrete optimization
- c. Goal programming
- d. Perturbation function

Guidance: level 1

:: Game artificial intelligence ::

An _____, also known as a heuristic _____ or static _____, is a function used by game-playing programs to estimate the value or goodness of a position in the minimax and related algorithms. The _____ is typically designed to prioritize speed over accuracy; the function looks only at the current position and does not explore possible moves.

Exam Probability: **Medium**

43. *Answer choices:*

(see index for correct answer)

- a. Transposition table
- b. Proof-number search
- c. Killer heuristic
- d. Arimaa

Guidance: level 1

:: Data clustering algorithms ::

A _____ or self-organizing feature map is a type of artificial neural network that is trained using unsupervised learning to produce a low-dimensional, discretized representation of the input space of the training samples, called a map, and is therefore a method to do dimensionality reduction. _____ s differ from other artificial neural networks as they apply competitive learning as opposed to error-correction learning, and in the sense that they use a neighborhood function to preserve the topological properties of the input space.

Exam Probability: **Low**

44. *Answer choices:*

(see index for correct answer)

- a. Single-linkage clustering
- b. Canopy clustering algorithm
- c. Nearest-neighbor chain algorithm
- d. Self-organizing map

Guidance: level 1

:: Support vector machines ::

_____ is an algorithm for solving the quadratic programming problem that arises during the training of support vector machines. It was invented by John Platt in 1998 at Microsoft Research. SMO is widely used for training support vector machines and is implemented by the popular LIBSVM tool. The publication of the SMO algorithm in 1998 has generated a lot of excitement in the SVM community, as previously available methods for SVM training were much more complex and required expensive third-party QP solvers.

Exam Probability: **Low**

45. *Answer choices:*

(see index for correct answer)

- a. Sequential minimal optimization

- b. Regularization perspectives on support vector machines

Guidance: level 1

:: Cluster analysis ::

In statistics, a _____ is a probabilistic model for representing the presence of subpopulations within an overall population, without requiring that an observed data set should identify the sub-population to which an individual observation belongs. Formally a _____ corresponds to the mixture distribution that represents the probability distribution of observations in the overall population. However, while problems associated with "mixture distributions" relate to deriving the properties of the overall population from those of the sub-populations, "_____ s" are used to make statistical inferences about the properties of the sub-populations given only observations on the pooled population, without sub-population identity information.

Exam Probability: **High**

46. *Answer choices:*
(see index for correct answer)

- a. Biclustering
- b. Mixture model
- c. Silhouette
- d. Medoid

Guidance: level 1

:: Markov models ::

In probability theory and statistics, the term _____ refers to the memoryless property of a stochastic process. It is named after the Russian mathematician Andrey Markov.

Exam Probability: **Medium**

47. *Answer choices:*
(see index for correct answer)

- a. Markov property
- b. GLIMMER
- c. Forward algorithm
- d. Examples of Markov chains

Guidance: level 1

:: Sensitivity analysis ::

_____ is the study of how the uncertainty in the output of a mathematical model or system can be divided and allocated to different sources of uncertainty in its inputs. A related practice is uncertainty analysis, which has a greater focus on uncertainty quantification and propagation of uncertainty; ideally, uncertainty and _____ should be run in tandem.

Exam Probability: **Low**

48. *Answer choices:*

(see index for correct answer)

- a. Sensitivity analysis
- b. Variance-based sensitivity analysis
- c. Tornado diagram
- d. Fourier amplitude sensitivity testing

Guidance: level 1

:: Control theory ::

_____ is the control method used by a controller which must adapt to a controlled system with parameters which vary, or are initially uncertain. For example, as an aircraft flies, its mass will slowly decrease as a result of fuel consumption; a control law is needed that adapts itself to such changing conditions. _____ is different from robust control in that it does not need a priori information about the bounds on these uncertain or time-varying parameters; robust control guarantees that if the changes are within given bounds the control law need not be changed, while _____ is concerned with control law changing itself.

Exam Probability: **Medium**

49. *Answer choices:*

(see index for correct answer)

- a. loop performance
- b. Damping

- c. process parameter
- d. state variable

Guidance: level 1

:: Data mining ::

In machine learning and pattern recognition, a feature is an individual measurable property or characteristic of a phenomenon being observed. Choosing informative, discriminating and independent features is a crucial step for effective algorithms in pattern recognition, classification and regression. Features are usually numeric, but structural features such as strings and graphs are used in syntactic pattern recognition. The concept of "feature" is related to that of explanatory variable used in statistical techniques such as linear regression.

Exam Probability: **Medium**

50. *Answer choices:*

(see index for correct answer)

- a. Conference on Knowledge Discovery and Data Mining
- b. Receiver operating characteristic
- c. Optimal matching
- d. GSP Algorithm

Guidance: level 1

:: Graph theory ::

A _____ is a stochastic model describing a sequence of possible events in which the probability of each event depends only on the state attained in the previous event.

Exam Probability: **Low**

51. *Answer choices:*

(see index for correct answer)

- a. Icosian calculus
- b. Chemical graph theory
- c. Mixed graph
- d. Domatic number

Guidance: level 1

:: Neural networks ::

In artificial neural networks, the _____ of a node defines the output of that node, or "neuron," given an input or set of inputs. This output is then used as input for the next node and so on until a desired solution to the original problem is found.

Exam Probability: **High**

52. Answer choices:

(see index for correct answer)

- a. Winner-take-all
- b. The Emotion Machine
- c. Activation function
- d. Tensor product network

Guidance: level 1

:: Mathematical optimization ::

In artificial intelligence, _____ is a technique of evolving programs, starting from a population of unfit programs, fit for a particular task by applying operations analogous to natural genetic processes to the population of programs. It is essentially a heuristic search technique often described as 'hill climbing', i.e. searching for an optimal or at least suitable program among the space of all programs.

Exam Probability: **Low**

53. Answer choices:

(see index for correct answer)

- a. Line search
- b. Basis pursuit denoising
- c. Cake number
- d. Genetic programming

Guidance: level 1

:: Machine learning ::

_____ is a subfield of machine learning in which multiple learning tasks are solved at the same time, while exploiting commonalities and differences across tasks. This can result in improved learning efficiency and prediction accuracy for the task-specific models, when compared to training the models separately. Early versions of MTL were called "hints"

Exam Probability: **Low**

54. *Answer choices:*

(see index for correct answer)

- a. Feature space
- b. Multi-task learning
- c. Predictive state representation
- d. Transduction

Guidance: level 1

:: Neural networks ::

In neuroscience and computer science, _____ refers to the strength or amplitude of a connection between two nodes, corresponding in biology to the amount of influence the firing of one neuron has on another. The term is typically used in artificial and biological neural network research.

Exam Probability: **Medium**

55. *Answer choices:*

(see index for correct answer)

- a. Optical neural network
- b. Synaptic weight
- c. Phase-of-firing code
- d. Grossberg network

Guidance: level 1

:: Computer vision ::

_____ is the extraction of meaningful information from images; mainly from digital images by means of digital image processing techniques. _____ tasks can be as simple as reading bar coded tags or as sophisticated as identifying a person from their face.

Exam Probability: **High**

56. *Answer choices:*

(see index for correct answer)

- a. Background subtraction
- b. Automated Imaging Association
- c. Image analysis
- d. Poisson image editing

Guidance: level 1

:: Game artificial intelligence ::

The _____, also known as the horizon problem, is a problem in artificial intelligence whereby, in many games, the number of possible states or positions is immense and computers can only feasibly search a small portion of them, typically a few plies down the game tree. Thus, for a computer searching only five plies, there is a possibility that it will make a detrimental move, but the effect is not visible because the computer does not search to the depth of the error.

Exam Probability: **High**

57. *Answer choices:*

(see index for correct answer)

- a. Computer poker players
- b. Horizon effect
- c. Computer Olympiad
- d. GADDAG

Guidance: level 1

:: Machine learning ::

_____ is a form of machine learning that exploits a very strong, or even perfect, domain theory in order to make generalizations or form concepts from training examples.

Exam Probability: **Medium**

58. *Answer choices:*
(see index for correct answer)

- a. Explanation-based learning
- b. Bias-variance dilemma
- c. Structural risk minimization
- d. Deep learning

Guidance: level 1

:: Operating system technology ::

An _____ , for the purposes of chronology and periodization, is an instant in time chosen as the origin of a particular calendar era. The " _____ " serves as a reference point from which time is measured.

Exam Probability: **High**

59. *Answer choices:*

(see index for correct answer)

- a. CPU shielding
- b. Epoch
- c. Working set
- d. System image

Guidance: level 1

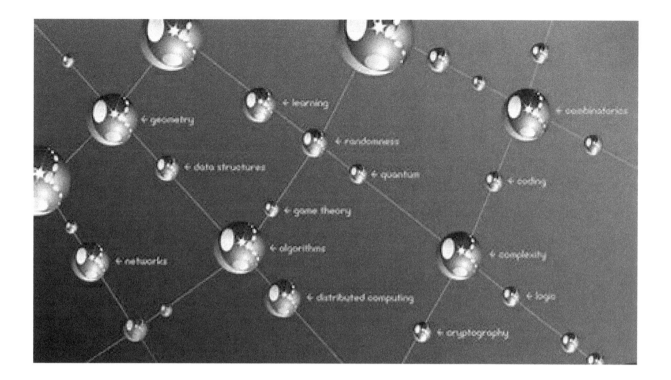

Computer networking

A computer network, or data network, is a digital telecommunications network which allows nodes to share resources. In computer networks, computing devices exchange data with each other using connections (data links) between nodes. These data links are established over cable media such as wires or optic cables, or wireless media such as WiFi.

:: Network architecture ::

An _____ is a type of optical telecommunications network employing wired fiber-optic communication or wireless free-space optical communication in a mesh network architecture.

Exam Probability: **Medium**

1. *Answer choices:*

(see index for correct answer)

- a. Optical mesh network
- b. Jump Server
- c. Next-generation access
- d. PCN Technology Inc.

Guidance: level 1

:: Ethernet ::

In computer networking, _____ physical layers carry traffic at the nominal rate of 100 Mbit/s. The prior Ethernet speed was 10 Mbit/s. Of the _____ physical layers, 100BASE-TX is by far the most common.

Exam Probability: **Low**

2. *Answer choices:*

(see index for correct answer)

- a. XAUI
- b. Xelerated
- c. Ethernet frame
- d. Fast Ethernet

Guidance: level 1

:: Physical layer protocols ::

In telecommunications, a _____ is an electronic device that receives a signal and retransmits it. _____ s are used to extend transmissions so that the signal can cover longer distances or be received on the other side of an obstruction.

Exam Probability: **High**

3. *Answer choices:*

(see index for correct answer)

- a. X.21
- b. Passband
- c. Repeater
- d. Synchronous serial communication

Guidance: level 1

:: Network protocols ::

PIP in telecommunications and datacommunications stands for Private Internet Protocol or _____ . PIP refers to connectivity into a private extranet network which by its design emulates the functioning of the Internet. Specifically, the Internet uses a routing protocol called border gateway protocol, as do most multiprotocol label switching networks. With this design, there is an ambiguity to the route that a packet can take while traversing the network. Wherein the Internet is a public offering, MPLS PIP networks are private. This lends a known, often used, and comfortable network design model for private implementation.

Exam Probability: **Medium**

4. *Answer choices:*

(see index for correct answer)

- a. Private IP
- b. Proxy Mobile IPv6
- c. Virtual circuit
- d. Netatalk

Guidance: level 1

:: Abstraction ::

_____ is the state or quality of being simple. Something easy to understand or explain seems simple, in contrast to something complicated. Alternatively, as Herbert A. Simon suggests, something is simple or complex depending on the way we choose to describe it. In some uses, the label "_____" can imply beauty, purity, or clarity. In other cases, the term may occur with negative connotations to suggest, a deficit or insufficiency of nuance or of complexity of a thing, relative to what one supposes as required.

Exam Probability: **High**

5. *Answer choices:*

(see index for correct answer)

- a. Intentional stance
- b. Hypostatic abstraction
- c. Simplicity
- d. Abstract structure

Guidance: level 1

:: Cryptography ::

In cryptography, _____ or cyphertext is the result of encryption performed on plaintext using an algorithm, called a cipher. _____ is also known as encrypted or encoded information because it contains a form of the original plaintext that is unreadable by a human or computer without the proper cipher to decrypt it. Decryption, the inverse of encryption, is the process of turning _____ into readable plaintext. _____ is not to be confused with codetext because the latter is a result of a code, not a cipher.

Exam Probability: **Medium**

6. *Answer choices:*

(see index for correct answer)

- a. MDS matrix
- b. Two-way security
- c. Signals intelligence
- d. Ciphertext

Guidance: level 1

:: Network architecture ::

A _____ is an identifier for a node or host on a telecommunications network. _____ es are designed to be unique identifiers across the network, although some networks allow for local, private addresses or locally administered addresses that may not be unique. Special _____ es are allocated as broadcast or multicast addresses. These too are not unique.

Exam Probability: **High**

7. *Answer choices:*

(see index for correct answer)

- a. Hop-by-hop transport
- b. R-SMLT

- c. Enterprise private network
- d. Multimedia telephony

Guidance: level 1

:: Internet architecture ::

In computer networking, _____ refers to a one-to-one transmission from one point in the network to another point; that is, one sender and one receiver, each identified by a network address.

Exam Probability: **Low**

8. *Answer choices:*
(see index for correct answer)

- a. Bufferbloat
- b. Routing table
- c. Unicast
- d. Quality of service

Guidance: level 1

:: Internet protocols ::

A _____ is a maritime commercial facility which may comprise one or more wharves where ships may dock to load and discharge passengers and cargo. Although usually situated on a sea coast or estuary, some _____ s, such as Hamburg, Manchester and Duluth, are many miles inland, with access from the sea via river or canal.

Exam Probability: **Low**

9. *Answer choices:*

(see index for correct answer)

- a. Text over IP
- b. Lightweight Access Point Protocol
- c. Port
- d. Media Gateway Controller

Guidance: level 1

:: Local area networks ::

_____ is the transfer of data over a point-to-point or point-to-multipoint communication channel. Examples of such channels are copper wires, optical fibers, wireless communication channels, storage media and computer buses. The data are represented as an electromagnetic signal, such as an electrical voltage, radiowave, microwave, or infrared signal.

Exam Probability: **High**

10. *Answer choices:*

(see index for correct answer)

- a. Serial over LAN
- b. Data transmission
- c. PhoneNet
- d. Token ring

Guidance: level 1

:: Fiber optics ::

An _____ is a flexible, transparent fiber made by drawing glass or plastic to a diameter slightly thicker than that of a human hair. _____ s are used most often as a means to transmit light between the two ends of the fiber and find wide usage in fiber-optic communications, where they permit transmission over longer distances and at higher bandwidths than electrical cables. Fibers are used instead of metal wires because signals travel along them with less loss; in addition, fibers are immune to electromagnetic interference, a problem from which metal wires suffer excessively. Fibers are also used for illumination and imaging, and are often wrapped in bundles so they may be used to carry light into, or images out of confined spaces, as in the case of a fiberscope. Specially designed fibers are also used for a variety of other applications, some of them being fiber optic sensors and fiber lasers.

Exam Probability: **Low**

11. *Answer choices:*

(see index for correct answer)

- a. Cable jetting
- b. Optical fiber
- c. Fiber optic nano temperature sensor
- d. Gradient-index optics

Guidance: level 1

:: Local area networks ::

_____ local area network technology is a communications protocol for local area networks. It uses a special three-byte frame called a "token" that travels around a logical "ring" of workstations or servers. This token passing is a channel access method providing fair access for all stations, and eliminating the collisions of contention-based access methods.

Exam Probability: **Low**

12. *Answer choices:*

(see index for correct answer)

- a. LAN switching
- b. Chaosnet
- c. Token ring
- d. Data transmission

Guidance: level 1

:: Network architecture ::

In computer networking and telecommunications, a _____ is a communication network which uses switching for connection of two non-adjacent nodes.

Exam Probability: **Low**

13. *Answer choices:*

(see index for correct answer)

- a. Interconnection
- b. IPoDWDM
- c. Switched communication network
- d. Collision domain

Guidance: level 1

:: Internet architecture ::

_____ is a method of remapping one IP address space into another by modifying network address information in the IP header of packets while they are in transit across a traffic routing device. The technique was originally used as a shortcut to avoid the need to readdress every host when a network was moved. It has become a popular and essential tool in conserving global address space in the face of IPv4 address exhaustion. One Internet-routable IP address of a NAT gateway can be used for an entire private network.

Exam Probability: **Low**

14. *Answer choices:*

(see index for correct answer)

- a. Route Views
- b. Network address translation
- c. Internet transit
- d. Quality of service

Guidance: level 1

:: Network topology ::

A _____ is a network topology in which each node connects to exactly two other nodes, forming a single continuous pathway for signals through each node - a ring. Data travels from node to node, with each node along the way handling every packet.

Exam Probability: **Medium**

15. *Answer choices:*

(see index for correct answer)

- a. Point-to-point
- b. Internet topology
- c. Ring network

- d. Feeder line

Guidance: level 1

:: Clients (computing) ::

In computing, a _____ is software that is acting on behalf of a user. One common use of the term refers to a web browser that "retrieves, renders and facilitates end user interaction with Web content".

Exam Probability: **High**

16. *Answer choices:*

(see index for correct answer)

- a. Client
- b. RUMBA
- c. User agent
- d. Game client

Guidance: level 1

:: Internet architecture ::

In computer networking a _____ , or routing information base, is a data table stored in a router or a networked computer that lists the routes to particular network destinations, and in some cases, metrics associated with those routes. The _____ contains information about the topology of the network immediately around it. The construction of _____ s is the primary goal of routing protocols. Static routes are entries made in a _____ by non-automatic means and which are fixed rather than being the result of some network topology "discovery" procedure.

Exam Probability: **Medium**

17. *Answer choices:*

(see index for correct answer)

- a. Routing table
- b. Multicast
- c. Internet traffic engineering
- d. OpenURL knowledge base

Guidance: level 1

:: Unified Modeling Language ::

On 19 July 1926, the Federal Capital Commission commenced operating public bus services between Eastlake in the south and Ainslie in the north.

Exam Probability: **Low**

18. *Answer choices:*

(see index for correct answer)

- a. Object-oriented software engineering
- b. Action
- c. Profile
- d. Reich Technologies

Guidance: level 1

:: Data modeling ::

An _____ in software engineering is a representation of concepts and the relationships, constraints, rules, and operations to specify data semantics for a chosen domain of discourse. Typically it specifies relations between kinds of things, but may also include relations with individual things. It can provide sharable, stable, and organized structure of information requirements or knowledge for the domain context.

Exam Probability: **Low**

19. *Answer choices:*

(see index for correct answer)

- a. Problem domain
- b. Compound key
- c. Information model
- d. Database integrity

Guidance: level 1

:: Mathematical structures ::

In mathematics, _____ is concerned with the properties of space that are preserved under continuous deformations, such as stretching, twisting, crumpling and bending, but not tearing or gluing.

Exam Probability: **High**

20. *Answer choices:*

(see index for correct answer)

- a. Ideal ring bundle
- b. Natural topology
- c. Vector space
- d. Topology

Guidance: level 1

:: Windows communication and services ::

In computing, <code> _____ </code> is a console application of some operating systems that displays all current TCP/IP network configuration values and refresh Dynamic Host Configuration Protocol and Domain Name System settings.

Exam Probability: **Low**

21. *Answer choices:*

(see index for correct answer)

- a. Windows Filtering Platform
- b. Indexing Service
- c. Windows DNA
- d. Ipconfig

Guidance: level 1

:: Computer security ::

In the fields of physical security and information security, _____ is the selective restriction of access to a place or other resource. The act of accessing may mean consuming, entering, or using. Permission to access a resource is called authorization.

Exam Probability: **Low**

22. *Answer choices:*

(see index for correct answer)

- a. Threat model
- b. Whitelist
- c. Ambient authority
- d. Access control

Guidance: level 1

:: Internet architecture ::

In networking jargon, the computers that are connected to a computer network are sometimes referred to as _____ s or end stations. They are labeled _____ s because they sit at the edge of the network. The end user always interacts with the _____ s. _____ s are the devices that provide information or services.

Exam Probability: **Medium**

23. *Answer choices:*
(see index for correct answer)

- a. classful
- b. End system
- c. Forwarding plane
- d. Core router

Guidance: level 1

:: Physical layer protocols ::

In telecommunications and computer networks, _____ is a method by which multiple analog or digital signals are combined into one signal over a shared medium. The aim is to share a scarce resource. For example, in telecommunications, several telephone calls may be carried using one wire. _____ originated in telegraphy in the 1870s, and is now widely applied in communications. In telephony, George Owen Squier is credited with the development of telephone carrier _____ in 1910.

Exam Probability: **Medium**

24. *Answer choices:*

(see index for correct answer)

- a. Gigabit Video Interface
- b. Multiplexing
- c. Polar modulation
- d. Subcarrier multiplexing

Guidance: level 1

:: History of the Internet ::

The _____ is an American nonprofit organization founded in 1992 to provide leadership in Internet-related standards, education, access, and policy. Its mission is "to promote the open development, evolution and use of the Internet for the benefit of all people throughout the world".

Exam Probability: **High**

25. *Answer choices:*

(see index for correct answer)

- a. Advanced Network and Services
- b. Internet Society
- c. Yandex Browser
- d. Glenn Davis

Guidance: level 1

:: Metropolitan area networks ::

A _____ is a computer network that interconnects users with computer resources in a geographic region of the size of a metropolitan area. The term MAN is applied to the interconnection of local area networks in a city into a single larger network which may then also offer efficient connection to a wide area network. The term is also used to describe the interconnection of several local area networks in a metropolitan area through the use of point-to-point connections between them .

Exam Probability: **Low**

26. *Answer choices:*

(see index for correct answer)

- a. UMTS-TDD
- b. Gigabit Chicago
- c. Open Transport Network
- d. Metropolitan area network

Guidance: level 1

:: Computer networking ::

A _____ specifies how routers communicate with each other, distributing information that enables them to select routes between any two nodes on a computer network. Routers perform the "traffic directing" functions on the Internet; data packets are forwarded through the networks of the internet from router to router until they reach their destination computer. Routing algorithms determine the specific choice of route. Each router has a prior knowledge only of networks attached to it directly. A _____ shares this information first among immediate neighbors, and then throughout the network. This way, routers gain knowledge of the topology of the network. The ability of _____ s to dynamically adjust to changing conditions such as disabled data lines and computers and route data around obstructions is what gives the Internet its survivability and reliability.

Exam Probability: **Medium**

27. *Answer choices:*

(see index for correct answer)

- a. Time-driven switching
- b. Fabric computing
- c. Physical media
- d. Routing protocol

Guidance: level 1

:: Malware ::

The _____ is a story from the Trojan War about the subterfuge that the Greeks used to enter the independent city of Troy and win the war. In the canonical version, after a fruitless 10-year siege, the Greeks constructed a huge wooden horse, and hid a select force of men inside including Odysseus. The Greeks pretended to sail away, and the Trojans pulled the horse into their city as a victory trophy. That night the Greek force crept out of the horse and opened the gates for the rest of the Greek army, which had sailed back under cover of night. The Greeks entered and destroyed the city of Troy, ending the war.

Exam Probability: **High**

28. *Answer choices:*

(see index for correct answer)

- a. Extended Copy Protection
- b. Flame
- c. Trojan horse
- d. Mobile code

Guidance: level 1

:: Cryptographic protocols ::

In computing, Internet Protocol Security is a secure network protocol suite that authenticates and encrypts the packets of data sent over an Internet Protocol network. It is used in virtual private networks.

Exam Probability: **Low**

29. *Answer choices:*

(see index for correct answer)

- a. X.509
- b. Renewable security
- c. Simple Authentication and Security Layer
- d. IPsec

Guidance: level 1

:: Modems ::

A _____ is a type of network bridge that provides bi-directional data communication via radio frequency channels on a hybrid fibre-coaxial and radio frequency over glass infrastructure. _____ s are primarily used to deliver broadband Internet access in the form of cable Internet, taking advantage of the high bandwidth of a HFC and RFoG network. They are commonly deployed in Australia, Europe, Asia and America.

Exam Probability: **Low**

30. *Answer choices:*

(see index for correct answer)

- a. Cable modem
- b. Satellaview
- c. Nano Ganesh
- d. Softmodem

Guidance: level 1

:: Mathematical logic ::

_____ is an arrangement and organization of interrelated elements in a material object or system, or the object or system so organized. Material _____ s include man-made objects such as buildings and machines and natural objects such as biological organisms, minerals and chemicals. Abstract _____ s include data _____ s in computer science and musical form. Types of _____ include a hierarchy, a network featuring many-to-many links, or a lattice featuring connections between components that are neighbors in space.

Exam Probability: **Medium**

31. *Answer choices:*

(see index for correct answer)

- a. Kripke semantics
- b. Epsilon calculus
- c. Structure
- d. Laver table

Guidance: level 1

:: Link protocols ::

In computer networking, _____ is a data link layer communications protocol used to establish a direct connection between two nodes. It connects two routers directly without any host or any other networking device in between. It can provide connection authentication, transmission encryption, and compression.

Exam Probability: **High**

32. *Answer choices:*

(see index for correct answer)

- a. Point-to-point protocol
- b. Frame check sequence

- c. Generic Stream Encapsulation
- d. Asynchronous Balanced Mode

Guidance: level 1

:: Computer network security ::

A _____ extends a private network across a public network, and enables users to send and receive data across shared or public networks as if their computing devices were directly connected to the private network. Applications running on a computing device, e.g. a laptop, desktop, smartphone, across a VPN may therefore benefit from the functionality, security, and management of the private network. Encryption is a common though not an inherent part of a VPN connection.

Exam Probability: **Medium**

33. *Answer choices:*

(see index for correct answer)

- a. Virtual private network
- b. Kerberos
- c. Fortinet
- d. IEC 62351

Guidance: level 1

:: File sharing networks ::

_____ computing or networking is a distributed application architecture that partitions tasks or workloads between peers. Peers are equally privileged, equipotent participants in the application. They are said to form a _____ network of nodes.

Exam Probability: **Medium**

34. *Answer choices:*

(see index for correct answer)

- a. Peer-to-peer
- b. TorrentPier
- c. Soribada
- d. Napster

Guidance: level 1

:: Data collection ::

A _____ is an utterance which typically functions as a request for information. _____ s can thus be understood as a kind of illocutionary act in the field of pragmatics or as special kinds of propositions in frameworks of formal semantics such as alternative semantics or inquisitive semantics. The information requested is expected to be provided in the form of an answer. _____ s are often conflated with interrogatives, which are the grammatical forms typically used to achieve them. Rhetorical _____ s, for example, are interrogative in form but may not be considered true _____ s as they are not expected to be answered. Conversely, non-interrogative grammatical structures may be considered _____ s as in the case of the imperative sentence "tell me your name".

Exam Probability: **Medium**

35. *Answer choices:*

(see index for correct answer)

- a. Mode effect
- b. IPUMS
- c. Unstructured data
- d. Question

Guidance: level 1

:: Network protocols ::

Data Over Cable Service Interface Specification is an international telecommunications standard that permits the addition of high-bandwidth data transfer to an existing cable television system. It is employed by many cable television operators to provide Internet access over their existing hybrid fiber-coaxial infrastructure. The version numbers are sometimes prefixed with simply "D" instead of " _____ ".

Exam Probability: **High**

36. *Answer choices:*

(see index for correct answer)

- a. Optical burst switching
- b. Fibre Channel over Ethernet
- c. Microcom Networking Protocol
- d. Sockets Direct Protocol

Guidance: level 1

:: Network analyzers ::

In computing, <code>_____</code> and <code>tracert</code> are computer network diagnostic commands for displaying the route and measuring transit delays of packets across an Internet Protocol network. The history of the route is recorded as the round-trip times of the packets received from each successive host in the route ; the sum of the mean times in each hop is a measure of the total time spent to establish the connection. _____ proceeds unless all sent packets are lost more than twice; then the connection is lost and the route cannot be evaluated. Ping, on the other hand, only computes the final round-trip times from the destination point.

Exam Probability: **Medium**

37. *Answer choices:*

(see index for correct answer)

- a. Xymon
- b. DSniff
- c. Packetsquare
- d. Nimsoft

Guidance: level 1

:: Information theory ::

In radio, multiple-input and multiple-output, or _____ , is a method for multiplying the capacity of a radio link using multiple transmission and receiving antennas to exploit multipath propagation. _____ has become an essential element of wireless communication standards including IEEE 802.11n , IEEE 802.11ac , HSPA+ , WiMAX , and Long Term Evolution . More recently, _____ has been applied to power-line communication for 3-wire installations as part of ITU G.hn standard and HomePlug AV2 specification.

Exam Probability: **Medium**

38. *Answer choices:*

(see index for correct answer)

- a. MIMO
- b. Information theory
- c. Relay channel
- d. Conditional mutual information

Guidance: level 1

:: Scheduling algorithms ::

_____ is a family of scheduling algorithms used in some process and network schedulers. The algorithm is designed to achieve fairness when a limited resource is shared, for example to prevent flows with large packets or processes that generate small jobs from consuming more throughput or CPU time than other flows or processes.

Exam Probability: **High**

39. *Answer choices:*

(see index for correct answer)

- a. Network scheduler
- b. Deficit round robin
- c. Fair queuing
- d. Lottery scheduling

Guidance: level 1

:: Channel access methods ::

Carrier-sense multiple access with collision detection is a media access control method used most notably in early Ethernet technology for local area networking. It uses carrier-sensing to defer transmissions until no other stations are transmitting. This is used in combination with collision detection in which a transmitting station detects collisions by sensing transmissions from other stations while it is transmitting a frame. When this collision condition is detected, the station stops transmitting that frame, transmits a jam signal, and then waits for a random time interval before trying to resend the frame.

Exam Probability: **Low**

40. *Answer choices:*

(see index for correct answer)

- a. Process gain
- b. Carrier sense multiple access with collision detection
- c. Near-far problem
- d. CSMA/CARP

Guidance: level 1

:: Transport layer protocols ::

In computer networking, the _____ is a conceptual division of methods in the layered architecture of protocols in the network stack in the Internet protocol suite and the OSI model. The protocols of this layer provide host-to-host communication services for applications. It provides services such as connection-oriented communication, reliability, flow control, and multiplexing.

Exam Probability: **Low**

41. *Answer choices:*

(see index for correct answer)

- a. TIPC
- b. Transport Layer
- c. Xpress Transport Protocol
- d. User Datagram Protocol

Guidance: level 1

:: Network performance ::

_____ is a bandwidth management technique used on computer networks which delays some or all datagrams to bring them into compliance with a desired traffic profile. _____ is used to optimize or guarantee performance, improve latency, or increase usable bandwidth for some kinds of packets by delaying other kinds. It is often confused with traffic policing, the distinct but related practice of packet dropping and packet marking.

Exam Probability: **Medium**

42. *Answer choices:*

(see index for correct answer)

- a. Best-effort delivery
- b. Verax NMS
- c. Bit error rate
- d. Flowgrind

Guidance: level 1

:: Network protocols ::

A _____ is a means of transporting data over a packet switched computer network in such a way that it appears as though there is a dedicated physical layer link between the source and destination end systems of this data. The term _____ is synonymous with virtual connection and virtual channel. Before a connection or _____ may be used, it has to be established, between two or more nodes or software applications, by configuring the relevant parts of the interconnecting network. After that, a bit stream or byte stream may be delivered between the nodes; hence, a _____ protocol allows higher level protocols to avoid dealing with the division of data into segments, packets, or frames.

Exam Probability: **High**

43. *Answer choices:*

(see index for correct answer)

- a. Protected Streaming
- b. Digital Media Access Protocol
- c. Apple Filing Protocol
- d. Fibre Channel over Ethernet

Guidance: level 1

:: Domain name system ::

A _____ is a computer application that implements a network service for providing responses to queries against a directory service. It translates an often humanly meaningful, text-based identifier to a system-internal, often numeric identification or addressing component. This service is performed by the server in response to a service protocol request.

Exam Probability: **Low**

44. *Answer choices:*

(see index for correct answer)

- a. TSIG
- b. OpenDNSSEC
- c. Name server
- d. Internet Provider Security

Guidance: level 1

:: Remote sensing ::

_____ is a computer model developed by the University of Idaho, that uses Landsat satellite data to compute and map evapotranspiration. _____ calculates ET as a residual of the surface energy balance, where ET is estimated by keeping account of total net short wave and long wave radiation at the vegetation or soil surface, the amount of heat conducted into soil, and the amount of heat convected into the air above the surface. The difference in these three terms represents the amount of energy absorbed during the conversion of liquid water to vapor, which is ET. _____ expresses near-surface temperature gradients used in heat convection as indexed functions of radio _____ surface temperature, thereby eliminating the need for absolutely accurate surface temperature and the need for air-temperature measurements.

Exam Probability: **Low**

45. *Answer choices:*

(see index for correct answer)

- a. WISDOM Project
- b. Photochemical Reflectance Index
- c. American Society for Photogrammetry and Remote Sensing
- d. METRIC

Guidance: level 1

:: Directory services ::

_____ is a directory service that Microsoft developed for the Windows domain networks. It is included in most Windows Server operating systems as a set of processes and services. Initially, _____ was only in charge of centralized domain management. Starting with Windows Server 2008, however, _____ became an umbrella title for a broad range of directory-based identity-related services.

Exam Probability: **Low**

46. *Answer choices:*

(see index for correct answer)

- a. X.500
- b. Lightweight Directory Access Protocol
- c. Active Directory
- d. Novell eDirectory

Guidance: level 1

:: Computer access control ::

_____ is the act of confirming the truth of an attribute of a single piece of data claimed true by an entity. In contrast with identification, which refers to the act of stating or otherwise indicating a claim purportedly attesting to a person or thing's identity, _____ is the process of actually confirming that identity. It might involve confirming the identity of a person by validating their identity documents, verifying the authenticity of a website with a digital certificate, determining the age of an artifact by carbon dating, or ensuring that a product is what its packaging and labeling claim to be. In other words, _____ often involves verifying the validity of at least one form of identification.

Exam Probability: **High**

47. *Answer choices:*

(see index for correct answer)

- a. Wilmagate
- b. Two-step verification
- c. Atomic authorization
- d. Authentication

Guidance: level 1

:: Network management ::

The Remote Network MONitoring MIB was developed by the IETF to support monitoring and protocol analysis of LANs. The original version focused on OSI Layer 1 and Layer 2 information in Ethernet and Token Ring networks. It has been extended by _____ 2 which adds support for Network- and Application-layer monitoring and by SMON which adds support for switched networks. It is an industry standard specification that provides much of the functionality offered by proprietary network analyzers. _____ agents are built into many high-end switches and routers.

Exam Probability: **High**

48. *Answer choices:*

(see index for correct answer)

- a. Common Management Information Service
- b. RMON
- c. HP Operations Manager
- d. Bipartite network projection

Guidance: level 1

:: Network layer protocols ::

In the seven-layer OSI model of computer networking, the _____ is layer 3. The _____ is responsible for packet forwarding including routing through intermediate routers.

Exam Probability: **Low**

49. Answer choices:

(see index for correct answer)

- a. MacIP
- b. JenNet-IP
- c. Network layer
- d. Internet Group Management Protocol with Access Control

Guidance: level 1

:: Network protocols ::

_____ is a standardized wide area network technology that specifies the physical and data link layers of digital telecommunications channels using a packet switching methodology. Originally designed for transport across Integrated Services Digital Network infrastructure, it may be used today in the context of many other network interfaces.

Exam Probability: **High**

50. Answer choices:

(see index for correct answer)

- a. Source-specific multicast
- b. STAMP
- c. Frame Relay
- d. Inter-server

Guidance: level 1

:: History of the Internet ::

_____ is a method of grouping data that is transmitted over a digital network into packets. Packets are made of a header and a payload. Data in the header are used by networking hardware to direct the packet to its destination where the payload is extracted and used by application software. _____ is the primary basis for data communications in computer networks worldwide.

Exam Probability: **Medium**

51. *Answer choices:*

(see index for correct answer)

- a. Federal Internet Exchange
- b. Commercial Internet eXchange
- c. Mozilla localizations
- d. Packet switching

Guidance: level 1

:: Home automation ::

A _____ is a serial assembly of connected pieces, called links, typically made of metal, with an overall character similar to that of a rope in that it is flexible and curved in compression but linear, rigid, and load-bearing in tension. A _____ may consist of two or more links. _____ s can be classified by their design, which is dictated by their use.

Exam Probability: **High**

52. *Answer choices:*

(see index for correct answer)

- a. Dynalite
- b. Home Automation, Inc.
- c. Electronics Design Group
- d. Vacuum cleaner

Guidance: level 1

:: Ethernet ::

_____ is a family of computer networking technologies commonly used in local area networks , metropolitan area networks and wide area networks . It was commercially introduced in 1980 and first standardized in 1983 as IEEE 802.3, and has since retained a good deal of backward compatibility and been refined to support higher bit rates and longer link distances. Over time, _____ has largely replaced competing wired LAN technologies such as Token Ring, FDDI and ARCNET.

Exam Probability: **High**

53. *Answer choices:*

(see index for correct answer)

- a. Chipcom
- b. PROFIenergy
- c. XAUI
- d. 10BASE-FB

Guidance: level 1

:: Compiler construction ::

In computer science, the _____ of data is its structure described as a data type, independent of any particular representation or encoding. This is particularly used in the representation of text in computer languages, which are generally stored in a tree structure as an _____ tree. _____, which only consists of the structure of data, is contrasted with concrete syntax, which also includes information about the representation. For example, concrete syntax includes features like parentheses or commas which are not included in the _____, as they are implicit in the structure.

Exam Probability: **Low**

54. *Answer choices:*

(see index for correct answer)

- a. Three address code
- b. Static single assignment form
- c. Abstract syntax
- d. Basic block

Guidance: level 1

:: Virtual reality ::

The _____ is the global system of interconnected computer networks that use the _____ protocol suite to link devices worldwide. It is a network of networks that consists of private, public, academic, business, and government networks of local to global scope, linked by a broad array of electronic, wireless, and optical networking technologies. The _____ carries a vast range of information resources and services, such as the inter-linked hypertext documents and applications of the World Wide Web, electronic mail, telephony, and file sharing.

Exam Probability: **Medium**

55. *Answer choices:*
(see index for correct answer)

- a. Rumble Pak
- b. Internet
- c. Next Limit Technologies
- d. Future Vision Technologies

Guidance: level 1

:: Packets (information technology) ::

_____ occurs when one or more packets of data travelling across a computer network fail to reach their destination. _____ is either caused by errors in data transmission, typically across wireless networks, or network congestion. _____ is measured as a percentage of packets lost with respect to packets sent.

Exam Probability: **Low**

56. *Answer choices:*

(see index for correct answer)

- a. Protocol data unit
- b. Packet loss
- c. Maximum segment size
- d. Fast packet switching

Guidance: level 1

:: Data types ::

In linguistics, a _____ is the smallest element that can be uttered in isolation with objective or practical meaning.

Exam Probability: **High**

57. *Answer choices:*

(see index for correct answer)

- a. Complex data type
- b. Signedness
- c. Void type
- d. Variable

Guidance: level 1

:: Holism ::

_____ characterises the behaviour of a system or model whose components interact in multiple ways and follow local rules, meaning there is no reasonable higher instruction to define the various possible interactions.

Exam Probability: **Low**

58. *Answer choices:*

(see index for correct answer)

- a. Theory of Colours
- b. Structured programming
- c. Holism in science
- d. Complexity

Guidance: level 1

:: Local area networks ::

A _____ is a computer network that interconnects computers within a limited area such as a residence, school, laboratory, university campus or office building. By contrast, a wide area network not only covers a larger geographic distance, but also generally involves leased telecommunication circuits.

Exam Probability: **Medium**

59. *Answer choices:*

(see index for correct answer)

- a. Traffic indication map
- b. Local area network
- c. Private VLAN
- d. Subinterface

Guidance: level 1

INDEX: Correct Answers

Foundations of Computer Science

1. a: Data integrity

2. b: Transport layer

3. a: Dynamic HTML

4. c: ManaGeR

5. c: Size

6. d: Analysis

7. : Debugging

8. a: Personal firewall

9. d: Operating system

10. a: Digital pen

11. d: Software development

12. : Wireless network

13. a: Thesaurus

14. a: MySQL

15. a: System file

16. b: Compact disc

17. a: Trackball

18. a: Toolbar

19. : Virtual reality

20. a: Multiplexing

21. : Column

22. c: Visual Basic

23. : Cryptography

24. a: Authentication

25. b: Output device

26. d: Volatile memory

27. d: Home network

28. c: Expansion card

29. b: Transaction processing

30. c: Applet

31. d: JPEG

32. a: Property

33. c: Computer

34. b: Network architecture

35. d: ROOT

36. b: Graphics tablet

37. d: Virtual machine

38. d: Document

39. c: Dialog box

40. : Network administrator

41. d: Adobe Photoshop

42. a: Local area network

43. b: Object-oriented programming

44. d: Hypertext

45. d: Executable

46. b: Top-level domain

47. c: Artificial intelligence

48. b: Trojan horse

49. b: Registered user

50. d: File Transfer Protocol

51. b: Internet

52. d: Graphical user interface

53. c: Memory module

54. a: Requirement

55. : Complexity

56. b: Space

57. b: Input device

58. a: Productivity software

59. : Diagram

Computers

1. c: Video capture

2. : PostScript

3. b: Dirty bit

4. : Random access

5. c: VistA

6. d: IP address

7. : Opcode

8. : Optical mesh network

9. b: SIMM

10. d: Symbol table

11. : Compiler

12. : Parity bit

13. b: Sense

14. d: Data compression

15. a: Internet traffic engineering

16. b: Instruction set

17. a: Barcode reader

18. d: Interrupt handler

19. d: Review

20. d: Datapath

21. c: Von Neumann architecture

22. d: Application layer

23. a: Structure

24. c: Frame Relay

25. a: PowerPC

26. d: Flag

27. : Memory address

28. d: Frequency modulation

29. a: Byte

30. : Instruction register

31. b: Memory address register

32. d: Linux

33. d: Network Layer

34. a: Apple

35. d: Combinational

36. b: Random-access memory

37. d: Vector processor

38. a: Arithmetic logic unit

39. c: Physical address

40. b: NAND gate

41. a: Instruction cycle

42. c: Input device

43. c: State diagram

44. b: Proxy server

45. b: Harvard architecture

46. c: Task manager

47. d: Register renaming

48. c: Superscalar

49. a: Shared memory

50. b: INI file

51. a: Control register

52. b: Direct memory access

53. a: IBM

54. b: File server

55. a: Multiplexing

56. a: Description

57. b: Symbol

58. : Computer architecture

59. c: Token ring

Human-computer interaction

1. : Rich user interaction

2. b: Contextual inquiry

3. : Paint

4. : Status bar

5. d: Bump mapping

6. b: Ubiquitous Communicator

7. : Input device

8. a: Web content

9. : Voice User Interface

10. d: TWAIN

11. d: Page view

12. b: User interface

13. : Netscape

14. d: Surface computer

15. b: Computer-aided ergonomics

16. c: Augmentation Research Center

17. b: Accessibility

18. b: Website promotion

19. d: Shopping directory

20. a: Adobe Photoshop

21. c: Heuristic evaluation

22. c: QR Code

23. a: SMART Board

24. c: Virtual user interface

25. b: Riding-like sitting

26. c: Information design

27. : Spatial file manager

28. d: VirtuSphere

29. a: Process-centered design

30. a: Samples per inch

31. d: Compositing

32. a: Speech processing

33. d: Blog

34. c: Sensorial transposition

35. b: Usability testing

36. a: Volumetric lighting

37. c: Separation of presentation and content

38. : Normal mapping

39. d: Voice command device

40. c: Conceptual model

41. b: Complex text layout

42. : Scrolling

43. : Sculpted prim

44. d: Plesk

45. c: Bookmark

46. d: Spyware

47. c: Web3D

48. a: Web scraping

49. : Virtual reality

50. c: Toolbar

51. : Design process

52. d: Single document interface

53. a: Virtual reality cue reactivity

54. d: VistA

55. b: Ty Girlz

56. b: ROSIDS

57. : Color vision

58. a: Debugging

59. c: U-Key

Software engineering

1. a: Assembly language

2. c: Control flow

3. a: Programming language

4. b: Paint

5. c: JPEG

6. d: Traceability

7. : Graphics

8. c: Structure chart

9. d: Tree traversal

10. c: Standard library

11. d: Local variable

12. a: Software system

13. d: Metadata

14. b: Sequence diagram

15. b: Concatenation

16. b: Function pointer

17. b: Namespace

18. b: Space

19. a: Text file

20. : Extreme programming

21. a: Message passing

22. d: Description

23. : Concept

24. b: Procedural programming

25. b: Schedule

26. b: Postscript

27. b: Semantics

28. : Pattern matching

29. a: Structure

30. : Integer

31. b: Mail

32. b: Byte

33. a: Input device

34. b: Unit testing

35. c: Central processing unit

36. b: Data validation

37. a: Search algorithm

38. c: Symbol

39. c: OpenGL

40. : Binary tree

41. d: Prolog

42. c: Sense

43. : Code

44. c: Gantt chart

45. b: Beowulf cluster

46. d: Role

47. b: Operator overloading

48. b: Artificial intelligence

49. : Assignment statement

50. d: Device driver

51. d: High-level architecture

52. d: Object code

53. c: Class diagram

54. b: Pseudocode

55. a: MySQL

56. : Insertion sort

57. b: Functional programming

58. : Identifier

59. c: Sequential access

Computer security

1. c: Code

2. : Information leakage

3. b: Dynamic Host Configuration Protocol

4. : Personal firewall

5. : Backup

6. c: Botnet

7. b: Quantity

8. d: Extranet

9. : Trusted Computing

10. d: Data mining

11. c: Brute-force attack

12. a: Peer-to-peer

13. b: Google

14. : Mobile code

15. d: Non-repudiation

16. d: InfraGard

17. d: Data link

18. c: Multilevel security

19. b: Cipher suite

20. a: Dictionary attack

21. a: CERT Coordination Center

22. b: Secure Hash Standard

23. c: Phishing

24. c: Payment Card Industry Data Security Standard

25. c: Vulnerability

26. : Transport Layer Security

27. d: Logic bomb

28. : Cisco Systems

29. d: Configuration management

30. b: Secure communication

31. d: Key exchange

32. : CompTIA

33. c: Discretionary access control

34. b: Wired Equivalent Privacy

35. b: Computer Fraud and Abuse Act

36. c: Authentication protocol

37. : War dialing

38. : Footprinting

39. b: Ettercap

40. : Promiscuous mode

41. a: Key distribution center

42. a: DMZ

43. a: Virtual private network

44. : Property

45. c: Certified Information Systems Auditor

46. b: Cross-site scripting

47. : Security management

48. a: Man-in-the-middle attack

49. b: Authentication

50. a: Encrypting File System

51. c: IDEAL

52. b: CRIME

53. c: Discrete logarithm

54. b: McCumber cube

55. : Password cracking

56. b: Threat

57. c: Building

58. b: Covert channel

59. a: Diameter

Theoretical computer science

1. b: Combinatory logic

2. c: Cascade algorithm

3. d: Association for Computational Linguistics

4. c: Context-free language

5. b: Differential evolution

6. c: Avida

7. d: Delaunay tessellation field estimator

8. c: Approximation

9. : Automatic sequence

10. b: Diff

11. d: CLC bio

12. b: Computation tree

13. a: CodonCode Aligner

14. : Discrete time

15. d: Backward chaining

16. c: Context-sensitive language

17. a: Artificial Intelligence System

18. : Autocatalytic set

19. d: Computer worm

20. a: Structure

21. d: Bioinformatics

22. c: Constructible function

23. a: Computational irreducibility

24. c: Entropy power inequality

25. b: Computational Sustainability

26. b: Reduced cost

27. a: Bi-directional delay line

28. : Asymptotic computational complexity

29. d: Fourier transform

30. d: Simplex algorithm

31. c: Abstract syntax tree

32. b: Abramowitz and Stegun

33. a: Poisson process

34. d: Artificial creation

35. a: Concurrency control

36. c: Bisimulation

37. b: Confidence interval

38. : Laplace transform

39. : Discretization error

40. : Semantics

41. : Markup language

42. d: Context-free grammar

43. c: Cylindric numbering

44. a: Halting problem

45. a: Lindley equation

46. c: Computational electromagnetics

47. d: Artificial chemistry

48. d: Discrete dipole approximation

49. c: Complexity class

50. c: X-Machine

51. c: Conference on Automated Deduction

52. c: Corecursion

53. c: Importance sampling

54. b: Goal programming

55. a: DNA computing

56. : Busy beaver

57. : Arbitrary-precision arithmetic

58. d: Genetic programming

59. d: Ambiguous grammar

Information technology

1. a: Asset

2. a: Information

3. d: Malware

4. d: Space

5. a: Electronic data interchange

6. b: Reference

7. a: Trojan horse

8. : Software as a service

9. c: Business intelligence

10. d: Data processing

11. c: Output device

12. c: Argument

13. d: Software

14. d: Compromise

15. d: Purchasing

16. c: Utility

17. d: Second Life

18. : Word Lens

19. c: Systems design

20. c: Html

21. : Artificial intelligence

22. a: Query language

23. d: E-commerce

24. d: Window

25. a: Virtual reality

26. a: File system

27. : Executive information system

28. : Visual Basic

29. d: Complexity

30. a: Data center

31. b: Management information system

32. a: Property

33. : Sense

34. : Balanced scorecard

35. b: BlackBerry

36. c: Project management

37. a: Transaction processing system

38. d: Customer relationship management

39. a: Experiment

40. a: IPhone

41. b: Evaluation

42. b: Supply chain

43. b: Structure

44. a: Spyware

45. d: Transport Layer

46. d: Private network

47. a: Random access

48. d: Information technology

49. : Role

50. a: Computer fraud

51. d: Knowledge management

52. c: Data mining

53. d: Manager

54. c: Best practice

55. b: Transaction processing

56. c: Library

57. b: IPad

58. d: Relational database

59. : Data dictionary

Database management

1. d: Space

2. c: Functional dependency

3. c: Data mining

4. b: Online analytical processing

5. c: Candidate key

6. a: IBM DB2

7. b: Two-phase locking

8. c: Database design

9. d: Asset

10. d: Sequential access

11. c: DAVID

12. a: Quality control

13. c: Reserved word

14. a: Time series

15. c: NewSQL

16. c: Superkey

17. b: Data store

18. b: Schedule

19. : Internet

20. d: Tablespace

21. c: Surrogate key

22. b: Sensitivity analysis

23. d: Data type

24. c: Database server

25. c: OLAP cube

26. c: Stored procedure

27. d: Data warehouse

28. d: Web server

29. c: XML schema

30. : Database application

31. c: Data security

32. c: Data integrity

33. c: Distributed transaction

34. b: Column

35. c: Markup language

36. : Relational database

37. : Simplicity

38. d: ROOT

39. : Referential integrity

40. : Dirty data

41. : Local area network

42. d: Data Definition Language

43. d: Access method

44. c: Data model

45. b: Embedded SQL

46. a: E-commerce

47. a: Serializability

48. b: Bitmap

49. : Perl

50. : Standard deviation

51. : Database schema

52. c: Reading

53. c: VBScript

54. a: Complexity

55. d: Data mart

56. c: Database security

57. : Performance tuning

58. : NoSQL

59. c: Oracle Database

Artificial intelligence

1. c: Error

2. : Logic programming

3. c: Nonlinear system

4. a: Outlier

5. c: Latent semantic analysis

6. b: Density estimation

7. d: Quantity

8. d: Horn clause

9. : Perceptron

10. a: Particle filter

11. a: Decision boundary

12. d: Random variable

13. d: Computational learning theory

14. b: Beam search

15. d: Loebner Prize

16. c: Heuristic

17. c: Optical character recognition

18. c: Edge detection

19. d: Backpropagation

20. d: Branch and bound

21. a: Artificial intelligence

22. a: Description logic

23. b: Importance sampling

24. a: GOFAI

25. a: Inverse kinematics

26. a: Semantic network

27. : Branching factor

28. a: Entailment

29. a: Hessian matrix

30. : Regret

31. : Semantic Web

32. a: Dynamic Bayesian network

33. : Predicate logic

34. b: State space

35. b: Advice taker

36. c: Hypothesis

37. c: Hamming distance

38. d: Belief propagation

39. a: Potts model

40. a: Search algorithm

41. a: Rule-based system

42. a: Least squares

43. : Evaluation function

44. d: Self-organizing map

45. a: Sequential minimal optimization

46. b: Mixture model

47. a: Markov property

48. a: Sensitivity analysis

49. : Adaptive control

50. : Feature vector

51. : Markov chain

52. c: Activation function

53. d: Genetic programming

54. b: Multi-task learning

55. b: Synaptic weight

56. c: Image analysis

57. b: Horizon effect

58. a: Explanation-based learning

59. b: Epoch

Computer networking

1. a: Optical mesh network

2. d: Fast Ethernet

3. c: Repeater

4. a: Private IP

5. c: Simplicity

6. d: Ciphertext

7. : Network address

8. c: Unicast

9. c: Port

10. b: Data transmission

11. b: Optical fiber

12. c: Token ring

13. c: Switched communication network

14. b: Network address translation

15. c: Ring network

16. c: User agent

17. a: Routing table

18. b: Action

19. c: Information model

20. d: Topology

21. d: Ipconfig

22. d: Access control

23. b: End system

24. b: Multiplexing

25. b: Internet Society

26. d: Metropolitan area network

27. d: Routing protocol

28. c: Trojan horse

29. d: IPsec

30. a: Cable modem

31. c: Structure

32. a: Point-to-point protocol

33. a: Virtual private network

34. a: Peer-to-peer

35. d: Question

36. : DOCSIS

37. : Traceroute

38. a: MIMO

39. c: Fair queuing

40. b: Carrier sense multiple access with collision detection

41. b: Transport Layer

42. : Traffic shaping

43. : Virtual circuit

44. c: Name server

45. d: METRIC

46. c: Active Directory

47. d: Authentication

48. b: RMON

49. c: Network layer

50. c: Frame Relay

51. d: Packet switching

52. : CHAIN

53. : Ethernet

54. c: Abstract syntax

55. b: Internet

56. b: Packet loss

57. : Word

58. d: Complexity

59. b: Local area network

CPSIA information can be obtained
at www.ICGtesting.com
Printed in the USA
BVHW011558220819
556561BV00003B/253/P